To dear Nan.

With Love & Good Wishes

for 1966

From Anne

IN TRUST AND TREASON

Suzanne Warenghem in her British uniform while training with the Special Operations Executive.

IN TRUST
AND TREASON

The Strange Story of Suzanne Warren

by

GORDON YOUNG

EDWARD HULTON

Published by E. Hulton & Co., Ltd.
161/166, Fleet Street, London, E.C.4.

Printed in Great Britain by C. Tinling & Co., Ltd.,
Liverpool, London and Prescot.

"Good neighbours I have had, and I have met with bad: and in trust I have found treason."

Queen Elizabeth, Speech to Parliament 1588.

To: The Three Musketeers

This *certificate* *is* *awarded* *to*

Mademoiselle Suzanne *Warenghem*

as a token of gratitude for and appreciation

of the help given to the Sailors, Soldiers

and Airmen of the British Commonwealth

of Nations, which enabled them to escape

from, or evade capture by the enemy.

Air Chief Marshal,
Deputy Supreme Commander,
Allied Expeditionary Force

1939-1945

CONTENTS

LIST OF ILLUSTRATIONS

ILLUSTRATIONS

9

ILLUSTRATIONS

FOREWORD AND ACKNOWLEDGMENT

FEW of the housewives somewhere in a London suburb standing with their shopping-bags beside a slim, auburn-haired young woman who is now the happily-married mother of two fine sons, know that she is also the heroine of one of the strangest of all the stories of the war. Few, even of Suzanne's Warren's closest friends have been shown the certificate which hangs in her little flat, signed by Lord Tedder, and thanking her for her secret work which enabled more than fifty allied fighting men to escape to Britain. And until now virtually nobody at all, except Suzanne's own husband, has known of the agonising human dilemma which her war-time gallantry brought her, one of the strangest personal ordeals, perhaps, experienced by any woman in time of either war or peace.

It was only after long hesitation that Suzanne Warren decided to allow me to tell her story in full and with considerable frankness. To enable me to do so she submitted herself, first in Paris as the welcome guest of my wife and myself, and later again in London, to long hours of questioning. She gave lively, helpful and always shatteringly-honest answers to an inquisition which must at times have been more than a little painful to her. Therefore it is, of course, primarily Suzanne Warren herself whom I have to thank for having made it possible for me to write this book.

But not all of her story could be told by Suzanne herself. Of some aspects her own modesty made her hesitant to speak; of others there were background features of which she did not even know. So it became necessary, over a period of many months, to conduct a process of detailed research among many of the people who had at different times been directly or indirectly associated with Suzanne. This was a task which took me to many parts of France, Belgium and Britain and introduced me to a large number of interesting and helpful people.

Among those who gave me every assistance in their power and whom I must certainly thank are Suzanne's two aunts Mdlle Isabelle and Mdlle Marie Bureau; her cousin Miss Lena G. Kemball, of Loughton, Essex; Monsieur L. Crépel, of Paris and his two daughters Jeanne and Francine; Mr. G. H. Darke, of Minehead; Dr. Albert Guérisse (Pat O'Leary) G.C., D.S.O.; Madame Carpentier, of Douai, mother of the heroic Abbé; Madame Deram-Vanhoutteghem of Loison-sous-Lens; Madame Francois Duprez of La Madeleine, Lille; Monsieur and Madame Galant of Roubaix; M. Roland Lepers of Garches; the Abbé Amy of Vincennes; M. Vladimir de Fliguë; the Rev. Donald Caskie, Minister of the Scottish Kirk in Paris; Dom Emmanuel, of the Benedictine Monastery at En Calcat; Mademoiselle de la Marguette of the "Bethanie" guest house; Mr. Robert Sheppard; Captain Paul de la Taille; M. Charles Warenghem; M. Jean Maurichaux Beaupré; M. George Croisé; M. and Mme. Roger Berthier, Mr. Ernest Swan, of Marcq-en-Barceul, and many others.

In particular, too, I must mention Mr. Vincent Brome, whose book "The Way Back" gives very fully the story of the escape organisation run first by Ian Garrow and later by Pat O'Leary; and M. Louis Nouveau, of Marseilles, who gave me permission to quote the letter from the Abbé Carpentier which had been communicated to him by Jean de la Olla, to whom it was addressed, and which is contained in his book "Des Capitaines par Milliers".

FOREWORD AND ACKNOWLEDGMENT

Finally both Suzanne and I must certainly acknowledge our debt for much helpful guidance to Miss Vera Atkins, whose invaluable work with Colonel Maurice Buckmaster during the war ought long ago to have been the subject of a book to itself.

Paris and Villars-sur-Ollon
1959

GORDON YOUNG

PART ONE

When Hearts were Young and Gay

"SUZANNE."

The lithe little brunette girl in the sandals and printed cotton dress took no notice of her father when he called to her.

"Suzanne, come down off that tree at once," he ordered— but the girl, her bare sun-tanned legs already chafed with climbing, resolutely went on scrambling up the tree.

"Suzanne, come in to the house, do you hear? If you're not a good girl, you know, Les Boches will get you."

Reluctantly the girl climbed down the tree and walked into the old untidy house, high up on the hill above the harbour of Le Havre.

"Les Boches." It was a familiar threat, the bogey-man of Suzanne's childhood, her father's stock final appeal. For years, because of it, the little girl used to dream at nights of being chased down dark, unending roads by Uhlan cavalrymen in spiked helmets, the kind which she had seen in her father's photographs of the First World War.

Suzanne's early life influenced her character greatly. She was born on November 22 (the same day of the month as General de Gaulle) in 1921 at Jouars-Pontchartrain, just outside Paris. Her family name was the northern French one of Warenghem, later anglicised to Warren by the British War Office during her secret war-time work. Her mother, a well-known local beauty from Nemours, died at the age of twenty-two when Suzanne was born, and the fact that she never knew her real mother cast a shadow over Suzanne's whole girlhood.

She was a pretty but wilful little girl, and there seems little doubt that it was her father from whom she had inherited her strong-willed ways; for Monsieur Warenghem was himself something of a character. He was half-English—his mother, before her marriage, had been a Miss Phoebe Ewing, of Woodford, Essex—and he was typically Nordic in appearance, of medium size, slim, with straight blond hair, pale blue eyes and light complexion. He had a fine baritone voice, and Suzanne used to love to hear him sing when she was a little girl. Throughout the first world war Monsieur Warenghem served with distinction, first with the cavalry and later with the infantry. He was gassed and was finally awarded the Croix de Guerre. All of which seemed to him reason enough to call the Germans for the rest of his life by the name which had survived from his soldiering days—Les Boches. He was still in uniform when he married in 1919 his beautiful bride, who became Suzanne's mother.

After demobilisation, Monsieur Warenghem became an agent for the French brewery firm of Karcher, but his heart was never in beer: his dream was to become a gentleman farmer. Finally he took the plunge, and went in for chicken-farming on a grand and ambitious scale. But his ambition was not matched by experience. The chicken farm failed, and with its disappearance went most of the family's savings. So finance was a problem in Suzanne's home from her very early days.

Normally mild and good-natured, Monsieur Warenghem was also extremely determined and hot-tempered, and he was capable of imposing his wishes in fits of overpowering rage. Once, returning home to find his bedroom in what he considered to be a state of excessive disorder, he flew into a frenzy and threw every article of linen and underwear within reach clear through the window and out into the garden. All through that morning the neighbours were astonished to see the rose-bushes of the

Warenghem home adorned with undervests, feminine brassières and other articles of intimate apparel.

Because of the death of her mother, Suzanne was sent, when she was only ten days old, to live with an aunt, the wife of her father's brother, in the Paris suburb of Asnières. Tante Jeanne —Madame Jeanne Warenghem—was typical of that kind of Frenchwoman who has always, through every crisis, remained the backbone of her nation. Small in stature, determined in character, brimming over with energy and ruthlessly stern when need be, she had a heart of gold, especially where children were concerned. Promptly and capably she took the motherless baby in hand, and her pleasure in watching the child develop into a pretty little girl was shared by her two unmarried sisters, the mademoiselles Marie and Isabelle Bureau. Between the three of them—Tante Jeanne, Tante Marie and Tante Isabelle—and Suzanne there grew up a bond of affection which was to last a lifetime and which was to have consequences which certainly none of them could have foreseen. Whenever Suzanne was in trouble it was to one of her aunts to whom she turned, and she never failed to find from them sympathy and help. Sometimes, too she went to spend happy holidays in the country with a fourth aunt, Tante Gabrielle, one of her father's two sisters who had a fine house at Thones, near Annecy. But Tante Gabrielle, who was Suzanne's godmother, moved to London before the war—and then aunts Jeanne, Isabelle and Marie became more important to her even than before.

Eventually Suzanne's father married for a second time, but, as is so often the case with second marriages, it took some time before the new wife and the child of the first marriage learned fully to understand each other. Monsieur Warenghem allowed Suzanne to grow up in the belief that her step-mother was her real mother, so that the occasional frictions between the two were particularly painful to the little girl. Then, browsing one day through an attic at home, Suzanne came across an old newspaper cutting telling of her father's first marriage to the lovely girl who had been her real mother, and she realised the truth. It was a shock to her—a shock that became a secret to be nursed only by herself. Suzanne for years never said a word either to her father or her step-mother about the knowledge that had come to her.

Right up from the time when Suzanne was a little girl her ties with Britain were extremely close. Apart from the fact of having an English grandmother, another of her aunts, Tante Germaine, her father's other sister, had married a wealthy Englishman, Mr. Joe Kemball, of Buckhurst Hill, Essex, and when Suzanne was only four and a half she made her first trip to England, to act as a bridesmaid at the wedding of their daughter. Another friend of hers, Miss Nancy Kemball, lived at Frinton-on-Sea, and Suzanne spent one long and lovely summer on those sunny sands playing with English children and learning to speak the language faultlessly. Those were the spacious days between the wars, Suzanne's relatives were comfortably off and her holidays, no doubt the most care-free days of her life, were passed in bathing, tennis and riding—and, of course, in endless childish chatter. One summer, too, Suzanne spent at a Girl Guides' camp near Caernarvon in Wales, and instantly felt at home in the atmosphere of good-comradeship which she found among the other girls there. "Those were the days when I first learned to love England," she once told me. It was a love which was to have far-reaching consequences.

A picture of Suzanne in those care-free days in England was given to me by her cousin Miss Lena G. Kemball, in a letter which she wrote to me from Essex. She says:—

"Suzanne stayed with us for the summer holidays every year from the time she was twelve until the year of the war . . . We knew one or two families near us with girls of the same age and they used to go out together, playing tennis or to the swimming-pool. . . .

"But if she was not with young people of her own age she

was quite contented to stay with the older ones. Sometimes we would go to the cinema, or occasionally up to London to visit some historical buildings, or she would go cycling.

"As a small child Suzanne was very stubborn; then, as a young girl she was rather an unusual character, older than her years and very reserved, although at times gay and excited. She was imaginative and romantic and a great reader. I remember on one occasion she said to me that she would like to have an exciting life. Well, she certainly had a few years which were more than exciting, and enough to last a lifetime!

"The last holidays Suzanne spent in England before the war were in 1938 at the time of the Munich crisis, and she was so hoping that if war broke out she would be unable to get back to France and have to stay in England. . . . I cannot say what she most particularly liked about England—perhaps the English blood in her veins had something to do with it."

*   *   *

Suzanne was about ten years old when she first went to live in the house in the Rue de l'Epargne, high above Le Havre, with her father, her step-mother and her two half-sisters, Paulette and Renée. She was a lively little girl, with regular features, abundant brown hair, sparkling blue eyes, and somewhat tomboyish tastes. She liked to run and shout and splash on the beaches of the Atlantic coast, but she had no use for dolls. Because of her own strong will, she frequently clashed with both her father and her step-mother, and her impetuous ways sometimes led her into harmless foolishnesses which caused her father to give her the affectionate nickname of "Ma Folle"— my madcap. She was full of girlish enthusiasms, an intense protagonist of causes. Thus, after one of her early visits to relatives in England, Suzanne returned to France so bemused by the British way of life that for weeks she insisted that her outraged French step-mother should drink tea daily for breakfast. "Everybody does it at Frinton," she explained with finality.

At Le Havre Suzanne attended first the Primary School and then passed without difficulty her examination for the High School, where she stayed for four years. Unlike many children, she enjoyed her school-days, for she was a good mixer, and enjoyed her studies too. She was good at every subject, save sewing and geography, and she was a keen reader, to the point of being something of a book-worm. She read everything she could lay her hands on, especially stories about Joan of Arc, who was one of the first of her early enthusiasms. She loved all books of travel and adventure and pored through the pages of Pierre Loti, Saint-Exupèry, Alain Gerbault the yachtsman who sailed alone round the world, and the great romantic writers such as Alexandre Dumas, Sir Walter Scott and Jules Verne. She was a born Romantic. By the time she was seventeen she was deep in the poems of Lamartine, Alfred de Musset, Villon and especially of Verlaine. One poem of Verlaine in particular had a haunting quality for her, written when he was looking out at a little bit of blue sky from the window of a prison cell:—

> Le ciel est, par-dessus le toit,
> Si bleu, si calme!
> Un arbre, par-dessus le toit
> Berce sa palme.

They were words which were to come back to her with strange appositeness before many years had passed.

In 1937 Suzanne left the High School of Le Havre, having passed the Brevet d'Enseignment Superieur, which gave her the right to work as a schoolteacher at the early age of only sixteen—a good year earlier than most other girls. But because she was judged too young to teach in school and because there were few openings of that sort in Le Havre, she was sent to a commercial college. In October 1938 the seventeen-year-old Suzanne got her first proper job, as temporary replacement to the Secretary of the Le Havre Lycée for boys. At the same time, studiously as ever, she worked to prepare herself for the Baccalauréat examination. Later she worked for a time as a secretary to a local attorney.

Suzanne was working too hard in those days to take much notice of politics, but at home her father was talking with increasing gloom of the prospects of another war. "It's those dirty Boches all over again," he bluntly declared. "Beat them once; now we'll have to beat them once more. Never mind, Gamelin's the man." (And had not General Gamelin, who was to be appointed Supreme Commander of the French and British forces, reported as late as the autumn of 1939 that the French army was "absolutely certain of victory if war were unhappily to occur"!)

And suddenly the war was there, though at first, of course, it was only a "phoney war". It did not interfere greatly with Suzanne's life, except that, because school-teachers were being called up to the French army, she was now offered, and accepted, a post as teacher in the local school of a village with the picturesque name of Melamare-Broche-à-Rotir (or Melamare-the-roasting-spit). Alas, it was at this point that Suzanne decided once and for all that she wasn't cut out to be a teacher. The village school was in a big ramshackle house standing far from other buildings in the remote Normandy countryside. At nights Suzanne was there all alone, and bitterly cold. By day some eighteen children between the ages of six and fourteen— and Suzanne herself was only four years older than the oldest pupils—turned up to be instructed and disciplined. She might have been able to do the former task, but she found herself quite unable to cope with the latter. The boys made jokes about her, and the girls giggled, so that the days of teaching were one long ordeal. And at nights the lonely old country house produced all sorts of unaccountable noises which were enough to keep any lonely eighteen-year-old girl from sleeping soundly. After three months of this, Suzanne thankfully accepted a chance to resume her former job as Financial Secretary at the Le Havre

Boys' School. She resumed her studies, too, and was due to take her final Baccalauréat examination in June of 1940.

But at the end of May, the first German bombs began to fall on Le Havre; on the afternoon of June 3 more than a thousand bombs were dropped on Paris in its first large-scale raid. Next day the Germans launched their decisive tank thrust towards Amiens, Péronne and Soissons. The real Battle of France had begun. Suddenly, everywhere in northern France, which had seemed so far from the war, there was talk of evacuation. Yet in Suzanne's house at Le Havre old die-hard Monsieur Warenghem was against any such nonsense. "No use being machine-gunned on the roads with a crowd of refugees," he told his wife and daughters. "Far better to be killed comfortably at home."

The German planes started sweeping low over the city, machine-gunning any civilians they could see in the streets. Once, when Suzanne was running to a shelter, a spray of bullets spattered down the street, missing her only by inches. After that she decided to stay in the house with her father.

But the raids soon got worse, and one brilliantly sunny June morning the French themselves set fire to the big petrol installations just outside Le Havre, to prevent the fuel falling into German hands. The thick black smoke from the blazing petrol slowly spread across the sky all over the city, turning the brilliant summer's day into sudden night. It was one of the most dreadful sights that Suzanne remembers of that period of the war.

All along the Rue de l'Epargne the houses were emptying, as more and more people evacuated the city. Only Monsieur Warenghem, still grimly defiant, hung on. But the time came when even he and his family at last had to go. One morning around noon sailors from the French navy came knocking at the doors of those civilians who still remained at home. "Get out—evacuate," they cried, "it's an order from headquarters." The sailors said that the roads leading out of Le Havre had been cut already and that the Germans were now in Rouen. The only way out of Le Havre was by fishing-boat across the estuary of the Seine.

"But Papa, what about the dogs?" pleaded Suzanne, as hastily the family packed together a few necessities to be carried on the journey. The two dogs, Mirette and Gipsy, were inseparable family friends.

"Sorry, we have to leave them behind," said Monsieur Warenghem. "I asked the sailors; we're not allowed to take them."

Quickly Suzanne ran down to the cellar and around the floor distributed all the pots and pans she could find, filled with food and water. Then she called Mirette and Gipsy, and gave each a hug of farewell.

Under the urging of the sailors, the family, including Paulette and Renée, hurried down to the harbour and scrambled on board one of the last fishing-boats to depart. Several had been sunk on the way across the estuary and Nazi pilots were still machine-gunning the rest. But Suzanne and her parents got across safely to the little port of Trouville, no longer a gay holiday resort but virtually an abandoned town, with only a few people remaining behind to help the refugees. They slept that night in an empty house in Trouville, and next day started off on the long trek down the dusty and dangerous roads, tramping along like all the other refugees and throwing themselves into ditches every time the German planes swooped overhead. Sometimes they got a lift for a little way, once in an army vehicle, once in a cattle lorry, and once, in Caen, from the municipal garbage truck. Some of the farmers had put up little stands alongside the road to supply the refugees with water, and now and then Suzanne stopped thankfully to drink. They slept at nights in fields or barns or in any shelter they could find. It was the story that was happening to families all over northern France.

For a whole week the family plodded on, until finally they came to the little Normandy village of St. Pierre-la-Vieille, where the Mayor was efficiently arranging billets for refugees who wanted to go no further. Suzanne and her family were put in an abandoned house, and there they thankfully decided to remain until it became more clear how events in France were developing. Nightly they gathered round the radio set which had been left behind by a previous owner. It was there that they heard with dismay that old Marshal Pétain had formed a new government in order to negotiate an armistice. And Monsieur Warenghem was incredulous and indignant when he listened to the announcement, on June 21, 1940, that the French representatives of the government had been received by Hitler to sign the armistice in the same railway carriage at Compiègne where that with Germany had been signed in 1918.

However, even in this hour of dismay, a remarkable thing was happening among the young people of France: they found it impossible to give up hope. All through those hot and disastrous days, the teenage boys and girls of the area, whom Suzanne quickly got to know, some of them local farmers' sons and daughters, some the children of other refugees, were gathering together in little groups to carry on, in any small ways they could think of, the struggle against the hated invader. Excitedly they listened on the radio to that famous first appeal of de Gaulle from London and cheered together when they heard him say "France has lost a battle, but France has not lost the war. . . . Our country is in peril, let us all fight to save it."

With her enthusiasm for causes and her long-standing love of England, Suzanne was in the forefront of the young people's drive. When there came streaming through the village stragglers from the dazed and demoralised French army, Suzanne eagerly helped the other youngsters to store the soldiers' rifles in secret hiding-places against the possibility of using them to good effect later on. When news came of French soldiers hidden in the fields and fearing capture by the advancing Germans, Suzanne was one of the first to take them food and civilian clothing. She helped Pierre, the Mayor's son, to watch for the movement of Germans and pass on the information wherever it would be most useful. Joyfully the young people on one occasion held one of their councils of war sitting on the wings of one of the last of the German bombers to be shot down in France, just before the capitulation. They did brave things and just foolhardy things, but at least their spirits remained resolutely unbroken. When the French national day of July 14 came around, one of the local farmers' boys took his father's car and carried a whole load of his friends, including Suzanne, into Caen, just to make a deliberate demonstration against the Germans. They all put red, white and blue favours in their lapels, made loud-voiced comments and laughed every time they passed a German soldier, went down to the river banks and sang the Marseillaise at the tops of their voices. The Germans, at that time still models of military "correctness", affected to take no notice of the exhuberant young people.

But such juvenile larks could obviously not for long satisfy Suzanne, with her overpowering sense of patriotism and her driving urge to be in the forefront of the battle for the two countries which she regarded as being almost jointly her own— France and Britain. She took a sudden and characteristically impulsive resolve. She would go herself to Britain, volunteer to join the forces of de Gaulle and show that even an eighteen-year-old girl could do something really useful to win the war.

It was a gallant, reckless, and obviously hopeless enterprise. But with high spirits and in good heart Suzanne slipped away one morning at dawn from the house at St. Pierre-la-Vieille, long before her parents were awake, and stole to the nearest main road, to hitch-hike her way south. She carried a coat over her arm, little else in her pockets and virtually no money; but the actual journey south was not too difficult. Some civilian cars were still on the roads and most drivers felt tempted to stop at the sight of a young, forlorn and pretty girl appealing for help. Now and then Suzanne found a bus or even a local train which was working and which took her still further on her journey, and finally she reached a village somewhere near Perpignan where, she had been told, there existed guides who were willing to take good patriots across the Pyrenees into Spain. Beyond that hint she had no information and no contacts, nor as her actions showed, much experience of the hard facts of life.

Suzanne walked in to the first café she could see and boldly asked if anyone could direct her to "the man who takes people into Spain". A tough mountain guide came up and when she explained to him her ambitions he simply laughed in her face.

"Ma petite," said the guide, "just how much money do you have in your purse?"

"About three hundred francs, I think," said Suzanne timidly. It was the equivalent of less than two pounds even at that time.

"Don't you understand, my little girl," said the man of the mountains, "that there are many people these days who would like to do that very trip. But it is neither easy nor safe—and it costs a lot of money—much, much more than three hundred francs."

"But it is for General de Gaulle," protested Suzanne. "Are you not a patriot?"

"A patriot perhaps—but not a philanthropist, Madamoiselle," shrugged the man, and abruptly turned away.

For several days Suzanne stayed on, eating little, to eke out her three hundred francs to the limit. But all the guides to whom she applied gave her similar answers, and finally she realised that her enterprise was hopeless. There was nothing for it but to give up, to go back again to father.

It was a very tired, hungry, disappointed and disillusioned young patriot who made her way wearily back to St. Pierre-la-Vieille—and also a very frightened little girl. Suzanne hardly dared to imagine what her father would say on her return. When at last she did encounter him again he burst into one of his moments of uncontrollable rage—perhaps the result of his long anxiety about the fate of his vanished daughter—and soundly slapped her face. Angrily he told her, "What in the world did you think you were doing—a young girl like you on the roads at a time like this? Anything could have happened to you. I'm not proud of what you've done—I'm ashamed of you, that's what I am. And how are we ever going to stop the villagers from hearing about it?"

Suzanne's only answer to her father was to burst into tears— but in the calm which later followed the storm she still believed that she had done the right thing in attempting to reach Britain. Strong-willed as ever, she quietly resolved that, when the right time and opportunity came, she would try again—only next time she would be more careful to make her plans aright. Among her intimate friends of "the gang" to whom she confided her story of her attempt to cross the Pyrenees, there was nothing but frank admiration for her pluck. But for many months after that first exploit, Suzanne's father kept an eagle-eyed watch on her.

Gradually, now, as Suzanne and her young friends met daily for eager gossip in the green fields of the Normandy countryside, the shape of defeated France was becoming clear. Under the terms of the armistice, to which Marshal Pétain had agreed, France was divided into "Occupied" and "Unoccupied" portions. The Germans controlled the whole of Northern France, from the English Channel to the Swiss frontier. The demarcation line between the two zones ran as far south as Tours, Bourges and Châlon-sur-Saône and took in the whole Atlantic coast, including Bordeaux. In all this area the Germans had full powers of control, short of the administration of local affairs. Only one-third of French territory, the "Unoccupied zone", remained in the hands of the government of Marshal Pétain which had been established at Vichy. And Vichy itself was a town of intrigues and divided counsels. On the one hand there were loyal French officials whose secret desire was still overwhelmingly to serve the allied cause. On the other, there was wide anti-British sentiment, fanned by Nazi propaganda that it was Britain who was responsible for France's downfall through having first urged her on to a hopeless struggle with invincible Germany and then abandoned her in her hour of need. And in between the two extremes were others who saw their duty to be that of conciliating their German conquerors, while at the same time resisting German efforts to use the remaining resources of France against their former allies. All the bitter controversies of the moment found their reflection in the excited discussions of the young people whom Suzanne met—and Suzanne never failed stubbornly to urge her friends that they should rally to the cause of General de Gaulle and, like her, make every effort to join the Free French forces which he was establishing in Britain.

But now, with the actual fighting over, there was no longer any point in the Warenghem family remaining evacuated, and at the end of the summer they all returned to their home in Le Havre, now fully in German hands. They were glad to be back again, and Suzanne was overjoyed when she found that the two dogs, Mirette and Gipsy, were safe and well, having been looked after by a kind-hearted neighbour who had returned to Le Havre before them.

The family's return to Le Havre came just at the moment when the Luftwaffe and the R.A.F. were beginning to fight out the Battle of Britain. Eagerly and with growing excitement Suzanne listened every night to the radio accounts of the mounting German losses.

But there was another side to this battle of the air which affected her more intimately. For new air raids began to take place on Le Havre—only this time they were not German but British planes which came.

Few people in Le Havre, that city which was later to suffer so grievously from the effects of allied bombardments, will forget the first day on which the R.A.F. came over on a bombing flight in force in that autumn of 1940. The droning of the engines and the crackle of the German flak brought everybody to their windows, and some people even to the rooftops, cheering the British planes, egging them on, shouting words of encouragement which, of course, were completely inaudible to the pilots above.

"Come on, la RAF," the people of Le Havre shouted, and with them, of course, Suzanne, "Viens vite, knock the Boches on the head, Vive l'Angleterre!" And above the roar of the engines, the bombs and the flak there swelled out from somewhere the words of the Marseillaise.

The Germans were furious at the demonstration, but there was nothing they could do about it, especially as the campaign for "friendship and understanding" between occupier and occupied was in full force just then.

Some of the British bombing, even though the Royal Air Force was so hard-pressed at this time, was exceedingly effective. Once, while Suzanne and her sister were watching from their window, the British planes scored a direct hit on a German ammunition train, which exploded with such violence that the two girls were lifted right off the floor. On another occasion, R.A.F. light bombers came over at night and lit up the city below Suzanne's home with parachute flares. In the light of the flares the British planes scored direct hits on the Le Havre Casino—just at the very moment when the Wehrmacht was giving an official ball there. Nobody ever knew who was the friend of the allies in Le Havre who had sent over to Britain the vital tip about that party. Every success of the R.A.F. merely served to whip up still further Suzanne's enthusiasm for the cause and to strengthen her determination to participate in the war herself at the earliest possible moment.

To this girl of intense enthusiasms and patriotic fervour the war had obviously brought something like a real emotional crisis. The state of nervous tension in which Suzanne was living at this time is illustrated by an incident which had an odd—and grimly humorous side. One day, while watching a British night raid on Le Havre from the window of her home, Suzanne saw one of the R.A.F. planes suddenly caught in a German searchlight—and writhing to escape. Helplessly and with her heart in her mouth, she stood at the window hoping against hope that the British pilot would escape, desperate at her own helplessness to assist him. Finally the German flak scored a direct hit on the plane, which crashed earthwards in a trail of flame and smoke. It was the first time that Suzanne had seen a British plane shot down, and she was very upset through her inability to do anything. The next day, purely from nervous tension, she developed a red rash which spread all over her body. A doctor gave her some ointment, but made it clear that the trouble was really of emotional origin.

Only a day or two later the Warenghems heard that, because of the good vantage point provided by their house, high up on the hill above Le Havre, a German observation officer was to be billeted on them. Once more Monsieur Warenghem was furious. "I won't have the devil in my own house," he said. "We've got to think of some way of getting out of it."

Accordingly when next day a Wehrmacht billeting officer turned up at the house to make the desired arrangements, it was Suzanne, her face covered in red spots, who was sent down alone to open the door. When she heard the German's mission she told him, with innocent eyes, "Of course your officer can come here if he likes—the only thing is that we are all suffering from some sort of disease—the doctors don't know exactly what it is, but they say it's frightfully contagious." The German soldiery never appeared at Suzanne's home again.

The bombing of Le Havre grew steadily more extensive and Suzanne's father decided that it was best to evacuate his family once again to the comparative safety of Paris, where his wife—Suzanne's step-mother—could stay with some of her own relations. This plan was tried for a while, but Madame Warenghem soon tired of it and decided that, after all, she would rather risk the bombings for the sake of being in her own home. So all preparations were made to return once more.

It was at this moment that Suzanne took a decision which was to affect profoundly the whole course of her life. She was still secretly determined to cross to Britain, but she knew that if she went back with the family to Le Havre and the watchful eye of her father, her chances of a second attempt at escape would become more remote than ever.

As usual, when in trouble, she went off to consult Tante Jeanne. "But you can stay here with me if you want to, Suzie," said her aunt. "We could try and get you fixed up with a job in Paris."

Because of her Commercial College training it was not long before Suzanne was able to find herself a suitable post—as a secretary in the Prefecture at Versailles. Promptly she wrote to her father telling him this news and imploring him to allow her to take the job and stay on in Paris with Tante Jeanne. To her delight, and slightly to her surprise, her father agreed, and in late November Suzanne moved into the flat in which Tante Jeanne was now living, in the Paris suburb of Becon-Les-Bruyères. Tante Jeanne welcomed her with open arms—and so did Tante Marie and Tante Isabelle, both living in the neighbourhood. None of them had any inkling of the strange drama in which Suzanne was to become involved within only a year, a drama which was to be played out, at least in part, in Tante Jeanne's respectable little second-floor flat.

* * *

Almost anything that Suzanne proposed the aunts were prepared to do, and gaily Suzanne christened them her "Three Musketeers". Nobody thought much about the consequences, for that was in the days before such words as Buchenwald and Dachau had revealed the full potential monstrosity of the Nazi mind. On some nights Suzanne and her three musketeers would go out armed with nothing more than a few pieces of chalk, and spend an hour or so in the black-out writing rude slogans about the Germans on any walls they could find unwatched.

They were not very brilliant slogans—"Tante Jeanne won't let me use some of the worst words I know," complained Suzanne—but they were the best the quartette could think of—"A bas les Boches", "Vive la France" and "Vive de Gaulle", and, even more easy to chalk up in a hurry, the "V" for Victory sign and the "✝" Cross of Lorraine, the symbol of the Free French forces. Usually Suzanne wrote while one aunt kept watch and another held a torch. Their proudest moment was the night they got one slogan up on the walls of a German barracks.

The gallant but elementary efforts of Suzanne and her three aunts to register their personal protests at the presence of the German invader in their beloved Paris were, in a sense, symbolic of what was happening among French people all over the country. For everywhere, and among all classes, there gradually formed, after the tragedy of Dunkirk and the Fall of France, little groups of people who even then remained strong in spirit and who privately resolved to carry on the struggle against the Nazis in any way they could. Their total numbers, compared with those who accepted defeat with stunned resignation, were at first not enormous, but they were the forerunners of the great movement which was to become known under the general term of the "French Resistance" and whose heroic activities not only vindicated the honour of France, but progressively came to play an increasingly important part in the liberation of their country. Gradually a whole series of Resistance "networks" came to be established under different code names all over France. Some were concerned mainly with aiding escapes from France, some with organising a regular flow of secret military and political information to the Allied Intelligence Services, and some with the extensive sabotaging of German communications and of French factories which had been forced to carry out work for the benefit of the Wehrmacht. As these resistance networks became more effective, so did the Germans intensify their efforts to hunt down the culprits and thousands of French

"THE THREE MUSKETEERS"

Tante Isabelle   Tante Marie   Tante Jeanne

Suzanne's three aunts who gaily risked their lives for four years during the German occupation.

onsieur and
adame George
arenghem,
zanne's father
d mother on
eir wedding
y in 1919. Her
other died
en Suzanne
was born.

"The 14th July" 1940: Sitting on the wing of one of the last German planes shot down over France before the Occupation, Suzanne (third from left) and some of her young friends on their way to Caen to stage a demonstration against the Germans.

Monsieur and Madame Crépel and their daughters Jeanne and Francine. They provided Suzanne with false papers for her escapees, their flat was always available to her resistance colleagues.

men and women perished as a result in concentration camps
or were shot as hostages. But no sooner was one network
destroyed than another arose to take its place, sending to Britain
by radio and by courier plans of German airfields, of Atlantic
Wall defences, of strategic targets to be bombed by the R.A.F.
or the American Air Force, and generally following in a multi-
tude of courageous and ingenious ways the call of General de
Gaulle and the summons of Winston Churchill to "set Europe
ablaze".

But these were early days and for the moment all that Suzanne
and her friends in Paris could do was to wage a sort of minor
"nerve war" of their own on the soldiers of the Wehrmacht in
the capital. Suzanne's colleagues among the secretaries in the
Versailles Prefecture used to cut out "V's" on sticky-backed
paper and plaster them wherever they could around the town.
Sometimes it even happened that a German soldier, coming
out of the crowded Paris Métro, would find one of the paper
V's stuck on the back of his coat. It was all very simple and childish and useless, of course, but it showed that even in defeated
France there were still hearts which were young and gay and
far from totally crushed. Such deeds were the forerunners of
the true Resistance, and it is good to remember that some
people in France, both very young and very old, were showing
such independence even at that early time when all the favours
of life seemed to be reserved for the collaborator and the black
marketeer.

All kinds of ingenious ways to bait the arrogant invader were
thought of by the circle of young people with whom Suzanne
was then associating. When first the incredible order came from
the Wehrmacht that all the Jews in Paris were to wear a yellow
star, many young French people who had not a trace of Jewish
blood in them promptly put on yellow stars. Then the Germans
had to enlarge their regulations, and make it equally punishable
for anyone to wear a yellow star who could *not* prove he was a
Jew. To guy the elegant Wehrmacht officers who went around

c

Paris with revolvers in shining black holsters, Suzanne's friends started the fashion of wearing a black belt to which was attached —a bicycle pump. In the Métro, they always ostentatiously turned their backs on the German soldiers, and one of Suzanne's girl friends had considerable success with a sharply-spiked umbrella which she managed with great regularity to stick "accidentally" into the backs of straphanging German soldiery.

The young friends devised jeering jokes to circulate in whispers against the Germans and one of them proudly produced what he termed the "New Alphabet of Occupied France", a punning play on letters which went, in part, like this:—

> La Nation—ABC (abaissé—brought down)
> La Gloire—FAC (effacé—blotted out)
> La France—OQP (occupé—occupied)
> Les Lois—LUD (éludé—evaded)
> Les Prix—LV (élevé—raised)
> Le Gouvernement—HT (acheté—bought)
> Mais—but
> L'Espoir—RST (resté—remained).

This document, too, was duly typed out, thirteen copies at a time, on the machines of Suzanne's civil service employer.

All this time Suzanne was saving every franc of her monthly salary that she could manage to hoard for the possibility of a new attempt to escape from occupied France to Britain. This was the one ambition which never left her mind, and which she even quietly confided to the trusted Tante Jeanne.

Then, one day at the Prefecture, Suzanne heard that a number of wounded British soldiers, officers and men, prisoners of war, were at a hospital in Paris, the Hôpital Bégin, near Vincennes. Promptly she resolved to visit them. "If I can't yet go to England," she told Tante Jeanne, "at least that's one small thing I can do. And anyway perhaps I'll find out from the soldiers some way I might be able to escape."

Suzanne collected a little bag of such delicacies as could still be found in the Paris groceries, as much as she could afford—a few dates, and a little cake to take to the hospital. She found the British soldiers lying in long rows on both sides of one ward of the hospital, and already a few other French people were visiting them. Suzanne saw one man who had lost his arm and who had nobody to talk to, so she introduced herself and gave him her little bag of delicacies. "Very nice of you, Miss, I'm sure," said the man—which is all that Suzanne remembers about that first conversation. She never knew the soldier's name; but he was the first of a long series of British soldiers whom Suzanne visited and it was these visits which in the end led her to her great adventure.

Through her regular visits to the Hôpital Bégin Suzanne made many new friends among French people who were doing the same as she was and who shared her patriotic views. Among them were Jeanne and Francine Crépel, two pretty daughters of a Paris business man. There was also a pleasant-faced Swiss woman, Madame Leblanc who, because of her relations in Switzerland, was able to secure more comforts for the British soldiers than most of the French sympathisers.

When Christmas came round in that grey grim year of 1940, the French visitors did everything they could to make it as happy as possible a time for the British soldiers. Miraculously, somebody found two big pictures of the King and Queen and a Union Jack, and these were hung prominently in the ward alongside a French tricolor. A visitor who was an expert in lettering produced a sign—"Merry Xmas to our Brave Allies"— and that was hung on the walls, too. The British were technically still prisoners of war of the Wehrmacht, but the hospital was run by French officials who closed their eyes to what was being done. A special sentinel was posted at the front gate of the hospital to warn those inside if any Germans should choose that day to inspect the British soldiers, so that the decorations could be hastily taken down. But no Germans appeared and there were toasts in French vin rouge and merry Anglo-French speeches.

However, one Sunday about two months after the Christmas festivity, Suzanne went to the hospital as usual only to find that all the British soldiers who had been there had suddenly disappeared. At first nobody would tell her what had happened to them: but in the end she found a nurse who was willing to speak. "They've all been shifted this morning," she told Suzanne. "They were taken to the Gare du Nord for transfer somewhere else. I think they may still be at the station."

Suzanne and twenty or more of her young friends, including the two Crépel girls, tore over to the Gare du Nord, and there, sure enough, was a trainload of wounded British troops. It was not possible at that period to buy platform tickets, so Suzanne and her friends spent their precious money on buying tickets to the next station down the line, in order to be able to pass on to the platform. There, under the noses of the uniformed Germans who were walking up and down the same platform, the British soldiers about to be deported to German prison camps and their young French sympathisers staged an enthusiastic Anglo-French demonstration such as would hardly have seemed possible in an occupied country in war-time. Crowding to the windows of their railway carriages, the wounded British soldiers in their uniforms, some of them looking still pale and sick, and some of them armless or legless, cheered and waved and shouted and gave the Cockney thumbs-up sign. The young people on the platform marched up and down shoutling loudly. "A bas les Boches," they cried, "Hope you get home soon", "Vive l'Angleterre," and "Vive la France". Scandalised, the watching German soldiers made an attempt to persuade the French demonstrators to leave the platform, but they did not use force, and they had little success. Finally the train moved off as those on the platform and those in the carriage joined together in a rousing chorus of "Pack up Your Troubles in your old Kit Bag".

The departure of this batch of British wounded left Suzanne and her friends at a loose end. When they went back to the Hôpital Bégin the following Sunday, hoping that another batch of British would have arrived, they found there only a solitary red-haired British private from Wolverhampton with an amputated leg. But a few weeks later, this soldier was transferred to the hospital of the Val-de-Grâce, near the Boulevard St. Michel, and so Suzanne and her friends switched their visits there. And only a week or so later a new and larger party of British troops turned up at the Val de Grâce, six officers and about forty men, nearly all of them men of the 51st Highland Division who had been casualties at St. Valery-en-Caux. All had just been transferred from Stalag 191 at St. Quentin, and were expecting later to be sent on to Germany.

Control of visitors at the Val de Grâce was more severe than at the former hospital, but Suzanne, who went there twice a week, on Wednesdays and Sundays, always managed to get in. Sometimes she posed as the fiancée of a French officer who was also an inmate of the hospital. Ostensibly she visited the Frenchman, then she always slipped down unobtrusively to the British ward.

Gradually, as she got to know the British soldiers better, Suzanne confided to them her secret ambition to escape to England. One of the British officers to whom she talked of her plans was a member of the Royal Army Medical Corps, Captain Geoffrey Darke. He told her in strict confidence that he and a fellow-officer, Lieutenant Kenneth Spreckley, of the Lothian and Border Yeomanry, and two others were already planning an escape, and he also gave her an address in Marseilles where, he believed, she might find somebody who could be trusted and might be a useful contact in helping her to cross the Spanish border. Suzanne agreed to smuggle out for Capt. Darke his medical instruments and some personal belongings, including photographs of his family and friends. She was thrilled with the feeling that at last she was playing a positive part in aiding, even in a small way, the escape of four British officers.

In fact, when the time came, Suzanne gave assistance to the four men which was invaluable. Years later, I wrote to Mr. G. H. Darke, who now lives at Minehead, asking him if he remembered his encounter at the Val-de-Grâce with Suzanne. He replied saying he remembered her perfectly, and he added—

"On the day of our escape we had to work to a close time-table, since we had to withdraw our parole, change into civilian clothes and make our escape in quick succession. This was planned to start at 6 p.m. and most unfortunately a party of Red Cross visitors arrived just prior to this. Suzanne was among them. In order to get rid of them and to keep to our programme, we told her what was happening and left her to find some way of getting them to leave without delay, which she did successfully. I do not know how she did it, as we did not see her again after the fun began."

The escape—which was successful—of Captain Darke and Lieutenant Spreckley and the two others merely intensified Suzanne's own determination to make the difficult journey to Britain as soon as she could. By this time she had saved a little money, though not much, and she thought it possible that she might be able to avoid paying a guide across the Pyrenees because of the address in Marseilles which Captain Darke had given her.

Then she made another lucky encounter—a French boy named Roger Pelletier who also came to the hospital regularly visiting the British soldiers. She liked him and trusted him and finally she confided to him her plan of escape.

"But Suzanne, I think I can help you there," said Roger. "I am only up here in Paris on leave. Actually I work at a Chantier de la Jeunesse down in the Pyrenees, not very far from the border. I know a priest who has a way of getting across

—and what's more I know how to get across the demarcation line from here into un-occupied France." (The Chantier de la Jeunesse was one of the Pétain government's organisations for young French people.)

Suzanne was delighted. "We'll go just as soon as ever you like," she told Roger. "And let's each of us take one English soldier with us—then we shall really be doing something useful."

So on her next visit to the Val-de-Grâce Suzanne approached one of the soldiers whom she knew best, a good-looking Sergeant from the 51st Highland Division named Tommy Edgar, and asked him, "What about us trying an escape to Britain? I think I know how we might be able to do it." When she explained her plan, Tommy jumped at it, and so did another Highlander named Jimmy Tobin to whom Roger made a similar proposition.

The four of them laid their plans with conspiratorial care. The first thing the two soldiers needed for their escape was a set each of civilian clothes. Suzanne secured these from the helpful Swiss lady Madame Leblanc. For Tommy the best she could provide was an old faded raincoat—a woman's raincoat at that—which was far too small for him, and a pair of baggy trousers. Because the buttons on the woman's raincoat were on the wrong side, Suzanne wore it into the hospital one day and gave it to the one-legged British soldier from Wolverhampton, who was an expert with needle and thread, and set him the task of changing the buttons for Tommy.

The trousers were a more difficult matter, because all packages taken to the hospital by visitors were examined at the gates. Suzanne solved this problem by putting on the trousers herself, tucked up uncomfortably under her skirt. Thus prepared, she marched boldly by the guard at the gate and began the walk across the wide courtyard of the hospital when a near-contretemps occurred. The trousers began to slip. At any moment, Suzanne felt, the hospital officials and the German troops wandering casually around might be surprised by the sight of a young French girl walking with long and obviously masculine trousers dropping to her feet from below her short and swinging skirt. With legs pressed close together, Suzanne just managed to reach the shelter of a doorway before the trousers finally cascaded around her heels. For Roger, of course, the problem was simple; he just put on the clothes for Jimmy Tobin underneath his own.

Now all was set for the escape. It was on a warm but dark June night of 1941 that the two British soldiers waited tensely in their ward until the hospital gradually grew quiet. They wanted to leave as late as they could, but had to make their escape before the last underground train left the nearby Métro station. Finally Tommy looked at his watch and said, "Let's go."

The two men made their way quietly to the hospital lavatory where they changed into their civilian clothes. Then they climbed out of the window, scrambled down a drainpipe, perilously crossed a glass roof which threatened to collapse under their weight, passed the hospital church, and finally jumped down into the yard at the back of a private house. It was from the front door of this house, in the nearby Rue des Feuillantines, that the two were due to emerge and there be met by Suzanne and Roger.

For what seemed hours the French girl and boy waited in the shadows of the street. It was pitch dark because of the black-out; and they were not sure from which of the doorways the soldiers were supposed to come out. As a precaution against sudden capture, they waited on the far side of the street so that, if Tommy and Jimmy were pursued by hospital guards, they themselves might have a chance of disappearing in the darkness. They peered anxiously into the darkness of the silent street, because the time was drawing near when the Métro would close down, and that was the only form of transport available to them for their escape. Moreover they must be away before the curfew.

At last they saw something moving out from a doorway across the road. It was Tommy and Jimmy. "Come on, quick," whispered Suzanne, grabbing Tommy by the hand, and the four of them rushed down the Rue des Feuillantines, swept round the corner into the Rue Nicole and just reached the Métro station as the last train was coming in. The odd-looking quartette dropped thankfully into their seats in the half-empty carriage—and then suddenly Suzanne began to laugh.

"Oh Tommy," she said, in a burst of uncontrollable girlish giggling, "you do look so funny."

And indeed the handsome British soldier, who in his hospital uniform had always appeared a model of military neatness, did look a strange, unkempt figure in his woman's converted raincoat many sizes too small, a French beret on his very Scottish-looking blond hair and the pair of old faded trousers hanging down over his shoes.

"Really, I don't see what there is to laugh all that much about," said Tommy a little huffily.

The good Madame Leblanc had promised to put up the party for the night, and when they reached her modern little flat near the Métro station Vaugirard they found that she had prepared a splendid feast for them, with special delicacies from Switzerland, and even a bottle of Champagne. Hungrily and merrily the fugitives sat down to celebrate the successful first stage of the escape.

Next morning there was a new problem to be tackled. Tommy and Jimmy must be provided with some sort of French identity cards if they were to have any hope of moving south through France in safety. The blank card itself could be obtained from any tobacconist, so Suzanne obtained two of these, and then she and Roger took the British soldiers off to a local photographer to have their identity-pictures taken. Neither of the two soldiers spoke fluent French, so when the photographer called out his directions—"De profil, s' il vous plait," neither of the men had the least idea what he was talking about, and

Suzanne had to try and show them by making frantic signs from behind. The photographer, with characteristic French tact, made no comment, but as they came away all four of the party agreed that he must have understood perfectly well what was going on.

Now came the problem of the official stamps, for it was no use putting the photographs on to the identity cards unless they were, in official fashion, half-covered by what would at least look reasonably like the legal stamp of some French authority. Because Roger had been a student of the Ecole des Beaux Arts, it was there that the party now proceeded to try and complete the identity cards.

Roger had read somewhere in a book that anything written in ink can be copied by taking the shell off a hard-boiled egg, pressing the egg on the ink, and transferring the impression to a piece of plain paper. With some difficulty Suzanne had produced an egg and anxiously the four of them gathered round as Roger pressed it firmly over the circular official stamp of his local Town Hall on his own identity card. Then he transferred the egg to Tommy's blank card and pressed it similarly over one corner of the photograph. Nothing whatever happened. The egg-idea simply didn't work. The amateur spies were baffled. So, while Suzanne pensively ate the hard-boiled egg, Roger went off to seek help. A few minutes later he came back with a new suggestion. A fellow-student had produced a rubber stamp of about the right dimensions which, in fact, belonged to the school Gymnastic Society. But at least in the middle of the stamp was the symbolical picture of Marianne, such as is used on many official documents, and so it was decided that this stamp would have to serve. Carefully obliterating the words "Societé de Gymnastique" with a piece of blotting-paper, and deliberately smudging the rest of the inscription on the stamp, Roger managed to produce something remotely resembling an official impression on both the identity cards.

"They look awful," said Suzanne frankly, "but they'll

simply have to do." In fact, no war-time escape was probably ever made with documents more clumsily forged.

After another night with the hospitable Madame Leblanc, the party left by train next day for Bordeaux. It was a reckless, happy journey, for all four of them were filled with a sense of elation over their adventure and were bursting with the high spirits of youth. There were German soldiers on the train, but they managed to find an empty compartment. Somebody produced a mouth organ and they all sang or hummed the popular tunes they knew.

It was a rather long journey but nobody was bored, at lunch-time, the four young people had a gay picnic discussing their plans for reaching England. Tommy and Jimmy hoped to rejoin their regiment and Suzanne to enlist in the French Free Forces. They reached Bordeaux without incident and changed into a local train for Langon, near the border of the line of demarcation into unoccupied France.

But at Langon there was a moment of near-crisis, only averted by Suzanne's presence of mind. As the party got out at the station, they saw with dismay that a German sentry had been posted at the exit and was checking every passenger's identity cards. He was scrutinising them with a close attention which seemed to make it virtually certain that the two British boys would never get past with their clumsily-forged papers.

Quickly, Suzanne thrust Tommy in front of her with Jimmy Tobin behind. Just as Tommy began handing his card, without speaking, to the German sentry, Suzanne pushed forward as though she was in a great hurry and put her own, genuine card, on top of Tommy's. Turning her big blue eyes on the German, she smiled at him sweetly and said in French, "Excuse me, Monsieur, but I'm a bit rushed to-day." And she went on talking rapidly to him while Jimmy came past from the rear and just flashed his card quickly before the sentry's eyes. The German was apparently so surprised at being smiled at by a pretty

French girl that he only beamed amiably back and let all four of them pass without comment.

Roger knew the way across the border from Langon. He led the party to a nearby saw-mill whose owner was a trusted friend. It stood right on the very edge of the border, which at that time was not marked by barbed wire or any fence but was simply under surveillance by a small German patrol. Roger asked his friend when the patrol has last passed by, and reported cheerfully to the others that they had a clear ten minutes in which to get across the border and into a neighbouring forest. With no trouble at all, the quartette just walked across to the comparative shelter of unoccupied France.

All through the night they walked on through the forest, singing loudly and laughing once they had got safely away from the border area. By about dawn they reached a village well inside Vichy-France and settled down to wait for the first train that would take them on to Toulouse and Labruguière, south of Castres, where Roger's Chantier de la Jeunesse camp was situated. They were tired, hungry and footsore after their long walk, especially the two British soldiers, whose shoes didn't fit them properly and whose feet had become raw and bleeding. The train was not due for several hours. So the party all settled down to sleep on the local war memorial.

The rest of the trip, as far as Labruguière, went so smoothly that it was more like a holiday than a war-time escape. The other young men of the Chantier de la Jeunesse gave an open-hearted welcome to the two British soldiers whom Roger introduced. The three of them stayed on at the camp for a week or so, while Suzanne slept in the village, but came up daily to eat her meals with the boys. Tommy and Jimmy needed a rest, and there were several warm June days spent happily by the quartette and their new-found friends in swimming in a nearby river, sunbathing and walking. Tommy Edgar had a good singing voice, and in the evenings he would lead the others in a camp sing-song, and, incongruously, from the camp which was supposed to be the very symbol of Vichy France, would sometimes come after dark the strains of "God Save the King" and the "Marseillaise".

But obviously such a situation could not last long, and one day the Commandant of the camp came and told the two British soldiers, "Sorry, but you'll have to go away. People in the village are beginning to talk."

Roger, of course, being a member of the camp, had to stay on. So Suzanne agreed to take Jimmy Tobin as well as Tommy Edgar down to Marseilles and try to find them—and herself— an escape route into Spain. It was no easy job for a nineteen-year-old girl to undertake. She had no experience of "resistance" work, no contacts, and when she and her two soldiers arrived by train at Marseilles station at seven o'clock one morning, after an all-night journey from Toulouse, she had exactly one hundred francs (about eleven and sixpence) in her pocket.

There was one anxious moment when the trio arrived at the Marseilles railway station—and once again the situation was saved by Suzanne's presence of mind. As the party walked down the platform from the train, a policeman in civilian clothes stopped Jimmy Tobin and asked him what was inside a package which he was carrying. The man spoke with a strong Marseilles accent, and Tobin was unable to understand a word he said. But before the policeman had time to notice that Tobin was a foreigner, Suzanne intervened, "We're travelling together —that's nothing but a few old clothes," and, with a dazzling smile at the detective she led the baffled Jimmy safely out of harm's way.

But now in Marseilles Suzanne had little idea exactly what to do next. First she went to the address which had been given to her in Paris by Captain Darke. But when she got to the number of the street he had mentioned she found that it was a large apartment house and she had no idea at which of the many front doors she ought to ring.

"I can't just go round to every flat and ask 'Are you the

people who help soldiers escape to Spain' can I?" she asked Jimmy and Tommy, and they both agreed that she could not.

The trio drifted around Marseilles that day rather disconsolately. They tried the consulate of the United States of America (then still a neutral country), but though an official there took particulars of Jimmy's and Tommy's regiment and so on, he said with regret that he could do nothing to help them escape. Later they met some kind of a British official who advised them frankly to give themselves up. "After all," he told the British soldiers, "as this is unoccupied France, you will only be interned and probably eventually repatriated." And he added, "But for this young lady here it will be much more serious for her to be caught aiding British soldiers to escape, as the Vichy-French police would certainly send her to prison."

When Jimmy and Tommy heard that, and as they walked together through Marseilles, they told Suzanne, "Obviously there's nothing for it but to give ourselves up, Suzie. We can't land you in a whole packet of trouble."

But self-willed Suzie would hear of no such thing.

"It's too ridiculous," she told the two soldiers. "Here we have come all this way, and got through everything with good luck everywhere—I just couldn't bear the thought of giving up now."

Then, all of a sudden, Suzanne remembered that Madame Leblanc in Paris had also given her the address of a man in Marseilles. He might be sympathetic, or he might have turned Pétainist, Madame Leblanc had warned, but she believed him to be a decent and honest man who in any case would probably not give them away to the police. So with this slender hope, Suzanne set off again, and found the man's office in the centre of Marseilles. Leaving the two British boys downstairs, Suzanne went up to the office alone, telling them that, if she was not back in half an hour, it would mean that something had gone wrong and they should go back to the American consulate and try again.

For ten minutes or so Suzanne sat in the Marseilles business man's office delicately sounding him out. She told him first merely that she had come to bring him greetings from Madame Leblanc. Then she turned the conversation to the war, to try and glean his general opinions. Finally, more from feminine intuition than from anything the man actually said, Suzanne decided that he was a person who could be trusted and she put her cards on the table.

"The fact is," she said, "I've got two British soldiers downstairs and I have no idea what to do with them. I can't take them to any hotel tonight because their identity cards are so bad that they would immediately be spotted by the police, and in any case I haven't got any money, either. Is there any chance you can find us a room, just for a night or two, while I try and find out how to get across into Spain?"

The business man, probably rather touched by Suzanne's youth and earnestness, at last broke into a smile and said, "Yes, actually it is possible that I may be able to help."

He rang for his secretary, who came in and explained that her brother, a priest, was running a home for down-and-outs in a suburb of Marseilles. She could fix it, she said, for the two British soldiers to sleep there, for at least a few nights.

Suzanne rushed downstairs to tell Jimmy and Tommy the news. "It's wonderful," she said with a laugh, "and anyway you two by now are so shabby you look as though you would just about fit in at a home for tramps." Ruefully, Jimmy and Tommy agreed that they did. So, accompanied by the secretary, they set out again, this time for the home for tramps. But on their way, pure chance intervened in a decisive manner. Just as the party was passing by the old harbour of Marseilles, Suzanne's eye was caught by a long, low, white building in the Rue de Forbin. Under the roof was a sign with the strange words "Omnium Isolation". And on the door, in unmistakable English was a notice which proclaimed, "British and American Seamen's Mission—now open to British civilians and seamen ONLY."

"Stop a minute," said Suzanne to the others. "Let me go in and explore."

Leaving the others in the street, Suzanne went inside the building. Somewhere in the distance a gramophone was playing a tune which dimly Suzanne recognised as the Scottish song, "By yon bonny banks. . . ." Two young boys were playing ping-pong.

"I'd like to see whoever is in charge here," said Suzanne, and a moment later a pleasant-faced clergyman came towards her.

It only took a few moments for the Scottish priest and the little French girl to realise that they could trust one another. For the priest was the Rev. Donald Caskie, Minister of the Scottish Kirk in Paris, himself a Highlander who had taken part in the mass exodus from Paris. In Marseilles he had taken charge of the Seamen's Mission and, at the behest of British Intelligence officials had turned this harmless-looking institute, despite its defensive label on the door, into a vital link of an escape route which helped to send hundreds of British soldiers across the Pyrenees into Spain. (The detailed story of his adventures has been told by Dr. Caskie in his own book, *The Tartan Pimpernel.*)

No sooner had Suzanne explained about the two British soldiers who were waiting in the street below than Dr. Caskie said cheerfully, "Bring them up." So Suzanne, Tommy and Jimmy bade farewell to the secretary whose brother had offered to provide shelter and gathered round Dr. Caskie to seek his counsel.

"I think I know just the man who can help you," Dr. Caskie told them. "And he should be coming along here any moment."

Little did Suzanne realise it at the time, but this was the encounter which was to turn her from merely being a patriotic and somewhat romantic young lady into a professional secret agent.

*　　*　　*

Standing Geoffrey Darke, and Kenneth Spreckley *third from left*. British officer prisoners in a military hospital in Paris; three of them and the one who took the picture escaped in May 1941. When a last minute hitch nearly upset their plan, Suzanne helped them.

Tommy Edgar   Jimmy Tobin

The first two men Suzanne took from Paris to Marseilles in June 1941. They were from the 51st Highland Division and had been taken prisoners at St. Valéry-en-Caux.

CARTE D'IDENTITÉ

Nom : *Le Gale*
Prénoms : *Aline Marie*
Profession : *néant*
Né le : *22 Novembre 1920*
à : *Bourg Blanc*
Département : *Finistère*
Domicile : *Guissony*
Finistère
Nationalité : *Française*

Le *14 Sept 1943*
SIGNATURE DU TITULAIRE,
A. Le Gale

SIGNALEMENT

Taille : *1 m 65*
Cheveux : *Chatain*
Yeux : *Bleus*
Moustache : —
Nez } Dos : *droit* Base : *normale*
Nez } Dimension : *Moyenne*
Visage : *ovale*
Teint : *Clair*
Signes particuliers : —

13 FRANCS
DA 2 FRANCS

Temoins,
Gamett
Le Blas

Le Maire
Commissaire de Police.

False identity card Suzanne used in 1944. She had changed her hair-do and appearance quite drastically as the Gestapo had circulated her description and photograph after her escape from prison.

Suzanne: Photo taken in Marseilles by a street photographer in 1941; she is carrying a spirit stove on which she cooked her meals in her small room.

Colonel Seagrim: Suzanne took him to Marseilles and freedom in September 1941.

The visitor who now appeared at the Seamen's Mission was a large, raw-boned man, rosy-cheeked and freckled, whose accent betrayed him immediately as an Australian. His name was Bruce Dowding, and he had lived for years before the war in the south of France, spoke perfect French and had now become one of the most active members of an escape organisation for British soldiers, which was operating successfully from Marseilles.

The organisation had been started, at first without official assistance and almost without funds, by Captain Ian Garrow, a powerfully-built and gallant survivor of the last stand of the 51st Highland Division at St. Valéry in the days after Dunkirk. In the summer of 1940 he had made his way south to Marseilles and might have himself escaped without difficulty across the frontier to Spain. But, struck by the plight of the flood of British soldiers still stranded in France, Captain Garrow had chosen to remain in Marseilles and organise an escape route for them. This finally became so efficient that shot-down airmen or escaping soldiers right up in the north of France and Belgium could be smuggled across the demarcation line and then across the frontier to Spain and Britain, sometimes within a matter of weeks. At this period Bruce Dowding was one of Captain Garrow's chief assistants in his escape organisation.

Rapidly Dr. Caskie explained to Dowding what Suzanne had told him, and introduced to him the two British soldiers.

"Yes, I can fix you up—all three of you," said Bruce. "Just come along with me."

Suzanne, Jimmy and Tommy bade farewell to Dr. Caskie and followed Bruce Dowding through the shabby streets of the Old Harbour to a quarter of the city which seemed even dingier and more sinister. They walked down a drab street which Suzanne noticed had the incongruous name of the Rue du Paradis, and finally turned into a house which bore an inconspicuous sign "Studios Meublés". It struck Suzanne as rather surprisingly clean, considering the district, and she was delighted when Dowding showed her a nicely-furnished room

49

D

on the ground floor with a large double bed and a basin with running water which she was to have for herself; Tommy and Jimmy were given another room on the first floor. Dowding gave the whole party supper, and that night Suzanne revelled in the luxury of clean sheets after her weary and anxious journey; she slept exceedingly well, being only slightly conscious of a certain amount of coming and going which seemed to be taking place in some of the other rooms of the house.

Next morning coffee and rolls were served to her in bed by a neat maid and Suzanne leisurely dressed, and wondered what was to happen next. She was only mildly surprised when, later that morning, as she was lying on her bed reading and feeling rather bored, the maid came in again and asked her, "Madmoiselle, would you be kind enough to go and join your friends in the room upstairs? There is a gentleman coming in this afternoon who needs this room for a little while."

Suzanne went upstairs and found Tommy and Jimmy just in the process of opening the shutters of their room and looking out into the street. Down below they saw Bruce Dowding carrying a package of what appeared to be food for them so they waved him a cheery greeting. A look of horror came over Dowding's face, and he hurried into the house.

"Close those shutters at once, you idiots," he commanded them. "Where the hell do you think you are?"

"I don't know," said Suzanne casually. "Some hotel or other, isn't it?"

"Of course it's not an hotel," replied Dowding, with irritation in his voice. "We couldn't possibly risk you all being in a hotel where the police might turn up at any moment."

"Where are we, then?" inquired Suzanne.

"In a Maison de Rendezvous, my dear little girl," said Dowding with a faint smile. "And if you are too young to know what that is, it's a place where a gentleman can hire a room for an hour or so at any time of day or night and spend it with his lady friend. There are no girls actually here; the gentleman brings his own. A very convenient arrangement, I assure you. Convenient to us, too, because the police almost never come here —they're afraid of finding somebody really important using the place."

"Strewth!" said Tommy. And Suzanne, to her intense embarrassment, felt she was suddenly blushing. At her home in Le Havre even the existence of such places had never been mentioned; and it seemed to her shocking beyond measure that now she had actually spent a night in one. When, later that morning, Bruce sent her out on some mission and she had to step from the door of the ill-famed house, she felt that everybody in the street was eyeing her.

Nevertheless the Maison de Rendezvous in the Rue du Paradis gave shelter to the three refugees for several nights more, until one day Bruce turned up again and announced, "It's all fixed— Sergeants Edgar and Tobin can start for the Spanish frontier tomorrow. Suzanne, I want you to take them to the Gare St. Charles and put them on the train. A guide will be on the train to take them to the Spanish frontier.

"But what about me?" asked Suzanne.

"Sorry, my dear," said Bruce, "but our organisation only deals with British soldiers, you know."

"You mean I'm to be left behind?" asked Suzanne in dismay.

"I'm afraid that's about it."

"But really," Suzanne protested, "one of the reasons why I've been to all this trouble was that I wanted to get to England myself to join the Free French forces. Surely you can't just drop me now?"

"I didn't say we were going to drop you, Suzanne," said Bruce Dowding. "Listen, it's like this. If you go to England and join de Gaulle you'll just be another person in the army. All very nice, of course—but if you stay with us in France you can do work that's fifty times more valuable. Do you realise that there are at this moment hundreds of British soldiers wandering around in France, and pilots constantly being shot down, all of whom we can help to get safely back home so that they can fight again. Most of these men don't know a word of French and badly need somebody like you to pick them up, guide them down to us, get them across the demarcation line, in and out of trains, and so on. You've done it once, now, with Edgar and Tobin, and done it very well, too. Do stay with us and carry on the good work—for both our countries' sakes."

And the freckled face of the big Australian broke into a persuasive smile.

"Well . . . if you really think I ought to . . ." said Suzanne a little doubtfully.

"Splendid!" said Dowding. "Then let's get cracking right away."

Suzanne next morning took Tommy and Jimmy to the station and with many farewell hugs and last-minute good wishes saw them off on the last stage of their escape.

Later that morning Suzanne moved from the house which had shocked her so much to a very ordinary little hotel where, of course, she was able to stay now that her soldiers had departed, since her own identity card was perfectly in order.

She saw Dowding again and he explained to her something— though at first not too much—of the work of the organisation. "You'd better stay here in the South with us for a while," he told her, "until you get to know the ropes."

At first Suzanne was entrusted only with a few small jobs, running errands, delivering messages, taking British soldiers across Marseilles. Once, when there was a report that a police raid was about to take place on one of the houses sheltering two British soldiers, Suzanne was sent to move the men quickly out of the way. She decided the safest place to hide them was at the cinema—so she spent the afternoon with them watching Jeannette Macdonald in *San Francisco* over and over again until it was safe for the men to go back to their hide-out late that evening.

Another of the early missions given to Suzanne after she had joined the organisation in Marseilles was an inquiry which had to be made in the prison of Clermont Ferrand. A member of the Garrow network had been caught and sent there—but nobody in Marseilles was certain how this had happened, whether it was a case of denunciation or whether it was sheer bad luck. The man's sister, Aggie, a pretty dark brunette, was in Marseilles, and Suzanne was asked to go with her to the prison to help get as much information on the arrest as possible. She agreed to pose as the fiancée of Aggie's brother.

When the two girls presented themselves at the Clermont Ferrand gaol, the authorities agreed to let them see the prisoner. As he was led by the guards into the interviewing room, Aggie said in a loud voice, "Look, your fiancée has come to see you, too," and Suzanne rushed forward, threw her arms round his neck and embraced him. The prisoner was sharp-witted enough to show not a trace of the surprise he felt. And, while Aggie flirted skilfully with the prison warder, Suzanne was able to carry on a whispered conversation with the prisoner. To anyone who did not hear the actual words spoken, it looked as though the two were exchanging terms of intimate endearment. But quickly Suzanne asked "What happened?" and succinctly the man was able to explain that he had been caught through sheer bad luck while crossing the border alone, that there had been no denunciation, and that he had had no British pilots with him when he was arrested. And that was exactly the information which the chiefs back in Marseilles had wanted to ascertain.

On another occasion Suzanne was sent to Lyons to conduct a British officer along the escape route to Marseilles. He was a Colonel Seagrim, whose home was in Farnham, Surrey, and he had, Suzanne was told, escaped from the Hôpital Cochin in Paris, where he had undergone an operation while a prisoner-of-war. A French network had helped him to escape and was taking him as far as Lyons where a member of that organisation, Jean Biche, would look after him until Suzanne arrived.

Suzanne travelled to Lyons, took over Colonel Seagrim from Jean Biche—and on the journey home nearly ran into serious trouble. It was not long after the invasion, in June 1941, of Syria by British Empire and Free French forces. Syria, which had been under the jurisdiction of the Vichy government, had been attacked by the Allies because it was being increasingly used as a base by the Germans, and in July General Dentz, the French High Commissioner, had applied for an armistice. Under its terms the French troops were offered service with the Free French forces or the alternative of repatriation to France. Events which seemed far away from Suzanne, but which now nearly involved her in trouble.

On the train from Lyons to Marseilles Suzanne took Colonel Seagrim to the Restaurant car for lunch; and they found themselves sitting at the same table as a French officer who had just chosen to be repatriated from Syria. He was bitterly anti-British and he started telling one of the other Frenchmen at the table stories of alleged British "atrocities" in Syria—how British officers had murdered their French prisoners, and other obvious fruits of Nazi propaganda. For a while Colonel Seagrim, who understood French well, and Suzanne both listened in silence to the officer's tirade. Finally the impetuous Suzanne could stand it no longer.

"You ought to be ashamed of yourself," she told the French officer. "To sit there spreading a lot of lies like that is just doing a traitor's job. Did you actually see any of the British atrocities yourself?"

"Well, no . . . not myself exactly," admitted the Frenchman.

"Then you shouldn't talk such nonsense," retorted Suzanne angrily.

Colonel Seagrim, discomfited by the whole unfortunate incident and also perhaps fearing that Suzanne might give away her true mission if she became over-excited, quietly tried to soothe her down. "Never mind, Suzanne," he whispered to her in French. "It really doesn't matter. I wouldn't go on like that if I were you."

But, once started, there was no holding Suzanne who, even in the Resistance was still, after all, the same girl whom her father had nicknamed "Ma Folle". She continued to tear into the French officer.

"For God's sake shut up, Suzanne," Colonel Seagrim whispered—but heedlessly Suzanne went on.

"How can you call yourself a soldier?" she taunted the Frenchman. "You were given the choice of fighting for France or of coming back here and living under the German jackboot like the rest of us—and you chose to give up the fight and come home. And just at the moment, too, when masses of French people are risking their lives every day in the Resistance. . . ."

The French officer by this time was growing almost apoplectic with rage, and Colonel Seagrim thought that matters had probably gone about as far as they could safely be allowed to go. Quietly he called for the waiter, paid the bill, and gently led Suzanne away from the dangerous encounter.

Back in Marseilles, Suzanne handed over the Colonel to Bruce Dowding, and he, too, eventually reached England safely.

Gradually, as she became more trusted, Suzanne met some of the other members of the organisation, Captain Ian Garrow himself, and a pleasant and gay young student named Roland Lepers, who was one of the pioneers of the organisation and was engaged in bringing escaping soldiers down from the extreme north of France. Then there was a charming and polished Greek journalist named Mario Prassinos, the grey-haired and distinguished Dr. Rodocanachi, Adolf, a Polish officer who was inevitably teased on account of his christian name, as well as many others.

A favourite gathering-place of the conspirators was a little Marseilles café called Le Petit Poucet, in the Boulevard Dugommier. One day while Suzanne was sitting outside the café in the sunshine sipping her favourite war-time drink, a "panaché"—half lemonade and half light beer—Bruce Dowding joined her with a stranger. He was a slim young Englishman, at least six feet tall, with a mass of thick blond hair, blue eyes, thin lips and a small blond moustache. He wore a well-pressed suit, carried himself confidently and greeted Suzanne with an amiable smile.

As the two men sat down at the table, Dowding said casually to Suzanne, "Here's our chief man up in the north, I don't think you've met him before. His real name is Harold Cole, though he's usually known as Paul."

PART TWO

Shadow of a Doubt

A<small>LTHOUGH</small> Paul Cole was destined to play such a vital part in the subsequent life of Suzanne Warren, she did not pay any particular attention to him on that day when they first met in Marseilles. To her he was just another member of Ian Garrow's organisation; she thought him pleasant-looking, he had a dashing air, and she was glad to hear from Bruce that he had already done much good work in bringing dozens of fugitive British soldiers down from Northern France to Marseilles and safety.

But if at that period—the summer of 1941—Suzanne had herself been in the northern part of France, she would have been more quickly impressed with the personality and the glowing reputation of Cole. For in that prosaic and forbidding area of coal mines and crowded industrial towns, of tram-cars and cobbled streets, between Amiens and the Belgian border, Cole's name was rapidly becoming a by-word for British chivalry, patriotism and courage.

Ever since the first world war, when French and British soldiers fought side by side through the horrors of the Battle of the Somme, no part of France has been more closely-linked with Britain than the extreme north, and in the days after Dunkirk and the French collapse, no French civilians showed themselves more steadfast in giving aid to British troops than those throughout all this region. It has been estimated that, just after Dunkirk, about one family in every ten in the area of Lille kept a British soldier hidden—and at least five other families knew about it, but never talked.

Therefore none of the good patriots of the north were in the least surprised when, in the autumn of 1940, there suddenly appeared among them—nobody quite knew where from—a charming and energetic Englishman who, speaking French with an obviously British accent, let it be known that he was a secret agent of the British Intelligence Service, a former Scotland Yard detective who had volunteered for the dangerous work of remaining behind the lines of the advancing German army and organising the escape of British troops. He told them of the contacts which he was able to maintain with London, and he gave vivid accounts of his exploits, of his narrow escapes from capture by the Germans, and of the two high Nazi officials whom he had already murdered on behalf of the British Secret Service. Within a few months the name of "le Capitaine Anglais" was being whispered with awe from Abbeville to Roubaix, and Paul Cole was drawing into his network a long and impressive list of courageous volunteers to help him in his underground work.

In Abbeville there was the tall and handsome priest, the Abbé Pierre Carpentier, who was also a French army reservist, and whose speciality was smuggling men across the river Somme. In Roubaix there were Monsieur and Madame L. Galant, who owned the mirror shop on the Rue de Lannoy, who fed and lodged more than fifty British soldiers brought to them by Paul, and sent them on their way south always with one thousand francs (£5.1.0) in their pockets, money which Madame Galant earned for them by working as a seamstress at nights. In Loison-sur-Lens there was a tiny, doll-like French girl named Madeleine Deram, who had gallantly sheltered Paul and many other British soldiers for months after Dunkirk. In the La Madeleine suburb of Lille there was an attractive woman hairdresser named Madame Vogglimaci, who courageously aided many of Cole's escaping soldiers. And also in Lille there was Monsieur Francois Duprez, who worked in the Mairie of La Madeleine. M. Duprez had a wooden leg and because he could not serve in the army gladly co-operated by supplying false identity cards for escaping allied prisoners. One of the first such cards he made was for Cole himself in the name of Paul Delobel, a common name in that area of France. And when Christmas of 1940 came around, Madame Duprez cooked a special dinner for the gallant British officer.

All these brave people, and scores of others too numerous to mention, became devoted workers for Paul Cole. When, years after the war, I spent a morning with the Galants of Roubaix, Madame Galant told me, "Everyone around here had the most complete confidence in 'Le Capitaine'. Some of my friends in the resistance used to tell me, 'If Paul ever quits we won't go on with all this dangerous work'. We all thought him 'un type trés chic'."

Cole's obviously British appearance helped his popularity, his manner inspired confidence. When he would say courteously, after receiving some service from a local patriot, "In the name of my King and Country I thank you", the recipient of his thanks felt a legitimate sense of satisfaction and pride.

Moreover Paul lived with a panache and an apparent disregard for danger which the French, with their natural love of drama, found irresistible. Madame Duprez told me, "He never seemed to have the slightest misgivings about his English accent. He went all around Lille freely among the German troops, sometimes on a bicycle, sometimes driving my husband's car—without a licence, of course. He sat among Germans in the cinemas, drank with them in bars, dined with his many girl-friends alongside Germans in the restaurants."

But sometimes, to avoid the necessity of directly speaking to the Germans, Cole used a document which he had typed out for himself in German certifying that he was deaf and dumb. Once, when Madame Vogglimaci had bought a stove to warm two British soldiers whom she was sheltering in her attic, the stove proved too heavy for her and Cole to carry into the house. Calmly Cole stopped two passing German soldiers, showed them the document, pointed to his own thin body—and the Germans obligingly carried up the stove!

But that was typical of Paul Cole in those days. Once, driving in a car from Valenciennes to Lille with Roland Lepers, Cole saw two Wehrmacht soldiers on the roadside seeking a lift. He stopped the car for them, and called to them airily in French, "Come on in, gentlemen—have a good time," and drove them in to Lille. And on another occasion, so Lepers once related to me, when Cole's car broke down it was he who stopped a Wehrmacht lorry and asked the driver authoritatively, "I say, mon cher, could you be kind enough to have a look at this engine for me?"

Not only Frenchmen, but British people too, placed complete reliance on Paul Cole. It was a Scotsman named James Smith, of Banffshire, who first introduced Cole to the Galants of Roubaix. Smith himself was a survivor from Dunkirk who had taken refuge in a French farm and spoke the local *patois* fluently. Another Englishman, Mr. Ernest Swan, of Marcq-en-Barceul, a veteran of World War I, also helped on Cole's escape route.

Down in the south the head of the escape line, Ian Garrow himself, had a high opinion of Cole. Paul turned up regularly in Marseilles, bringing with him consignments of British soldiers who were full of praise for the way in which he had conducted them south.

As for Suzanne, busying herself with the various assignments as they were given to her, she saw Cole at first only occasionally, and made no special effort to see him more. In any case it was an open secret in the organisation that Cole had a girl friend in Marseilles. He had a taste, which he never attempted to conceal, for good food, fine wine and glamorous women. He was at his best seated at a dinner-table surrounded by such things, relaxed, talking easily, in a low voice and impressively, though with a show of modesty befitting an English gentleman, of his past exploits as a secret service agent. Even in war-time

France it was possible nearly everywhere to find a cosy black-market restaurant with a dinner almost up to pre-war standards, provided you had the money to pay for it. And sometimes Paul had, it seemed.

Then, one day at the beginning of September 1941, Ian Garrow summoned Suzanne to meet him at the café. It was an unusual summons, for "the Chief", for obvious security reasons, did not meet his agents more than he could help; many of them, including Suzanne, had no idea where he actually lived. But that fateful morning, Garrow told Suzanne, "Look, my dear you have done well for us while you have been here, and now I've got a job for you which is much more important than anything you have done yet. One of our agents in the north has been arrested and we need somebody to take his place. Would you be willing to go back to the occupied zone and work for us there? It's a dangerous job, obviously, but you could help us enormously if you would do it."

Without a moment's hesitation Suzanne agreed. It was just what she had been longing for—the chance to play a greater, more exciting part in the organisation.

"That's fine, then," said Garrow. "You'll work with our man who's in command in the north and in Belgium—but then you have met him already, I think—Paul Cole. I'd like you to go north with Cole and Roland Lepers just as soon as you can get away."

When Cole met Suzanne again he said, "I hear we're working together now. I'm sure we'll get along splendidly."

Only a few days later Suzanne, Cole and the gay student Lepers left Marseilles together for the north. It was an uneventful trip and the ease with which the journey went seemed to augur well for the future. The trio took a train to Toulouse and from Toulouse to Loches, near the frontier of the unoccupied zone. From there a friendly farmer took them in his cart to a spot where they were fetched by a farmer from the other side of the line and taken to the little village of Bleré. Thence they took a train to Tours, and a few hours later they found themselves in Paris.

Cole and Lepers had their own "safe houses" in Paris, places where they could hide-out without danger of being denounced. So Suzanne went to stay with her Tante Jeanne at Becon-les-Bruyères. In the course of their work Paul often used to come and see her there, and, to explain Paul's outlandish French accent, Suzanne told her aunt that he was an American journalist and that she was acting as secretary to him. Whether she believed this or not, good Aunt Jeanne was careful never to ask Suzanne any embarrassing questions. "I do hope you'll be careful what you do, my dear," was the most she ever said.

In the weeks that followed, of course, Paul and Suzanne were increasingly thrown into each other's company, and Suzanne, twenty years old and incorrigibly romantic, was both flattered by Paul's tactful attentions and impressed by her new role as the chief assistant to a British officer of high repute. Moreover she was fired with enthusiasm for their common cause. At long dinners to which Cole invited her and which went on until late in the evenings, Suzanne would develop at length her favourite theme, that although some French people had given up the struggle, many more wanted still to fight back and that neither in spirit nor in fact was France truly beaten. And in his quiet, sympathetic voice Cole would agree with everything she said. "My dear, you are absolutely right," he would tell her. "It is just wonderful what you are doing."

One of the first places to which Cole took Suzanne was a big brasserie on the edge of Les Halles, called the Chope du Pont Neuf. Here the tall, slim and grey-haired proprietor, Monsieur Eugene Durand, who had himself served throughout the first world war, had established a regular service for feeding the British soldiers and shot-down pilots who were passing through Paris on their escape-route south. Batches of the men, tired and hungry after their journey, and sometimes as many as a dozen at a time, would sit on the long, red-plush banquettes at the rear of the brasserie, silently eating the good food which somehow or other M. Durand and his wife, who presided at the cash desk, always managed to provide for them, but seldom asked to be paid for. Often there were German soldiers eating in the front part of the restaurant or drinking at the bar, and M. Durand always treated them with perfect courtesy, for he regarded their presence as a sort of protection for the British soldiers in the back. And he always warned his British guests, "Eat, drink and keep quiet. If you must talk say 'oui' or 'non', but never anything else." And the hungry soldiers were only too glad to agree, as Durand's two trusted waiters, M. Elie and M. Georges Croisé, silently and efficiently served them.

Cole introduced Suzanne to M. Durand and told him, "She's one of us now. She'll probably be bringing you quite a lot of guests." And M. Durand welcomed her with a smile.

"First rate chap, that," Cole told Suzanne over a drink at the copper-topped counter. "Known him for years. When I was a small boy my mother, who was widowed, used to bring me to Paris and we stayed at a little hotel just across the street. I was an only child, you know—and I was very fond of my mother. Anyway, that was when I first got to know M. Durand —and that was when I started to learn French, of course."

In the weeks that followed Suzanne was introduced by Cole to several other members of the northern part of the British escape network. There was small, quick-witted Vladimir de Fliguë, a friend of Durand, who ran a little factory for making electrical resistances in the Rue de Quatrefages, just near the Jardin des Plantes, and whose home provided a "safe house" for British soldiers. There was Professor Fernand Holweck of the Radium Institute of Paris, whose great ambition, like Suzanne's, was to get to Britain, where he believed that his scientific knowledge would be of service to the allied cause.

One day Paul Cole arrived at Aunt Jeanne's house with the Abbé Carpentier from Abbeville, and the two took Suzanne out with them to lunch at the Chope du Pont Neuf. "I've brought the Abbé down specially so that you can meet each other," Paul told her. And he explained that the Abbé's work was particularly important because he was in the "zone interdite", the area north of the Somme which was even more rigorously controlled by the Germans than the rest of the occupied zone, and because of his contacts with other priests in that area. When a British pilot was shot down in northern France, he was usually at once hidden by the local farmers. And the first person to whom the farmer would turn to for advice on what to do with the pilot was usually the local priest. He it was who could put the man into direct contact with the Abbé Carpentier—and thus start him straight on the way home to Britain. The Abbé found food and civilian clothes for the men, manufactured false identity cards for them, and saw them safely across the river Somme. On that ocasion of their first meeting he asked Suzanne if she knew anybody who could help him reproduce the official stamps of the local German Headquarters. She did—and Professor Holweck produced two convincing stamps for the Abbé on gelatine.

In Paris, too, Suzanne sometimes took Paul Cole to lunch with her friends the Crépel family. The parents of M. Crépel had come from Roubaix, which Paul knew well, and they had mutual friends there. As M. Crépel told me after the war, "We always in those days found Cole *très sympathique*. He was not exactly good-looking, but he had a very pleasing manner— and one which completely turned the heads of women." To which M. Crépel's two daughters, Jeanne and Francine, agreed.

The Crépels learnt from Cole that he had served as a British officer throughout the Belgian campaign, and they had such confidence in him that they never hesitated to secure identity cards from a friend of theirs who worked in a local Mairie, and pass them on to Suzanne for Cole.

So, all through that autumn of 1941, Suzanne's life fell into a kind of routine of new and intriguing adventure. Up in the "zone interdite", Paul Cole, Roland Lepers and their loyal friends would collect the British soldiers and dispatch them, through the Abbé Carpentier, as far as Paris. There it was the task of Suzanne to meet them at the Gare du Nord, and take them—in small groups to avoid attracting attention—in the Métro to the Chope du Pont Neuf to be fed, and then on to some safe house to spend the night. The next morning Suzanne, usually with Paul Cole, would accompany the soldiers on the train from Paris to Tours. In Tours Cole and the men—in number anything from three to a dozen—would spend a few hours in another safe house, while Suzanne would travel on to the little village of St. Martin-le-Beau, right on the fringe of the unoccupied zone. There, long before, Roland Lepers had arranged with a patriotic Frenchman, M. Besnard, to act as the organisation's secret agent for getting the men across the demarcation line. M. Besnard himself was engaged in dredging the river Cher, and he knew every inch of that part of the border between occupied and unoccupied France.

Suzanne would check each time with M. Besnard that all was in order for another trip and that there had been no "trouble" since the last one. Then, she would walk back from St. Martin-le-Beau, along the banks of a small tributary of the River Cher, towards the village of Azay. This was part of a special "security plan" devised by herself and Cole. Paul, with the soldiers from Tours, would get out of the train at Azay and nonchalantly go for a stroll along the river bank. If they met Suzanne on the path they knew that all was well. If they did not meet her, they would have known that something had gone wrong, and would be able to escape in time. And if, indeed, there had been trouble, Suzanne would have been the only one to have been arrested at St. Martin-le-Beau, and, being alone, would have had at least a reasonable chance of being able to talk herself out of trouble. Naturally it was a dangerous mission, but Suzanne accepted the risk in a spirit of high adventure. Once, when she saw a German patrol on a bridge over the river, she took refuge under a hay-cart. Then, to her horror, she saw Paul and three British soldiers coming down the tow-path. Her instinct was to cry out a warning to them—but she realised that would only attract still further the attention of the Germans. Paul himself saw the Germans only after it was too late for concealment. So, with characteristic assurance, he kept on in a swinging walk down the river path—and the Germans took no notice of him and his three companions. "Quite a narrow squeak, what?" he afterwards said, with a smile.

When the party reached M. Besnard's house, he would give them all a hearty meal. Then, at dead of night, he would take them out and set them on their way across the border. From there on Cole knew the route and the party would walk all night until, around dawn, they were met by another farmer, now in the Free Zone, who fed them and sped them on their way to the village of Loches. Usually it was around six o'clock in the morning when they arrived in Loches, to wait an hour or two for the grindingly slow and totally unheated local train that took them into the nearest town of Châteauroux. Never, felt Suzanne, has one girl made so many hideously uncomfortable journeys. The cold and dirty war-time trains seemed to have square wheels, so slowly did they go. In Châteauroux there was a chance to have lunch before catching the next train to Toulouse, where they would arrive around nine o'clock in the evening. The waiting-room at Toulouse had been taken over by some Vichy organisation, so there was nothing for the travellers to do but sit around on the ground on the windy platform waiting for the midnight train that would take them on the all-night journey to Marseilles. The train was always packed, and often Suzanne and the rest of the party would have to spend the night standing in the dimly-lit corridor, pressed tightly in among the swaying crowd of sleepy fellow-travellers. The British escapers were always warned never to talk in the trains. But one night, one of the soldiers, as the train jolted round a bend, stepped heavily on the foot of an old lady just behind him. "Oh,

I beg your pardon," said the soldier, involuntarily and very audibly in English, his British good manners getting the better of his caution. The old lady smiled sympathetically, and the other bystanders in the corridor preserved an ostentatious silence.

The whole trip from Paris to Marseilles thus took—when all went smoothly—just over two days—a period of anxiety, danger, intense physical discomfort and very little rest. When the party arrived at last at Marseilles, Suzanne usually went straight to her little hotel room, threw herself down on her bed and slept for twelve or more hours at a stretch. She made five trips of this sort between September and the end of November 1941, accompanying in all about thirty-five British soldiers. But when the party got to Marseilles, it was always Paul who took charge of handing over the soldiers to Ian Garrow or Mario Prassinos or another member of the organisation. "Now you needn't worry any more, my dear, you can leave it all to me," he told Suzanne. "I'll do the actual handing over; it's better that way."

The trips back to the north from Marseilles were sometimes even more rugged than the journeys from north to south, and on one of them Paul and Suzanne had a hairbreadth escape from capture.

For some reason Paul was in a hurry to get back, but when they reached the demarcation line the farmer who was due to meet them was not to be found. "Never mind," said Cole. "Let's go on anyway, I'm pretty sure I know the route."

At the farm they found a young French soldier from Pétain's army who was also trying to get across the border because he was anxious to go on leave to Paris—without a pass. The three decided to join forces.

It was a bitterly cold and dark November night, and rain was pouring down as the trio set off for the all-night walk which would take them in the direction of St. Martin-le-Beau. They walked in single-file, but it was so dark that it was almost impossible to see the person immediately in front. They knew that the whole area was crawling with German patrols who would not hesitate to shoot on sight. Even the best of guides would have been hard put to it not to get into trouble that night. At one point they came to a wide highway which it was necessary to cross. The French soldier went first, before any of the trio realised that his heavy army boots would make a clatter on the road that could be heard far away. And heard it was, by a German patrol car which happened to be standing only a few yards down the road. Immediately a searchlight from the car flashed over the rain-sodden fields and there were guttural cries of "Achtung! Halte."

Just before the searchlight swung round to them, Paul and Suzanne rushed up a bank by the side of the road and flung themselves in the muddy field at the top. Suzanne got entangled in a barbed-wire fence which ripped her dress and her legs. For what seemed hours, they lay on their faces in the mud, while the rain lashed all around them and the German searchlight swung just over their heads.

Finally the Germans gave up the search. Dripping and shivering, Suzanne, Paul and the French soldier stood up and tried to take their bearings in the pitch darkness. Holding hands now, and stepping gingerly, they made their way towards where they believed lay the path along the river Cher. They knew that the river was somewhere near—so near, indeed, that they were in danger of walking right into it. So Paul drew coins from his pocket and started throwing them ahead of him into the darkness. When he heard one of the coins land with a splash they knew they were at last by the river.

Nearby they found a farm-house—a strange one whose occupants they did not know. But they took a chance and knocked at the door and the farmer's wife let them go inside and clean themselves up.

"No one could say we exactly look our best for paying calls," said Paul with a wry smile. Their clothes were drenched, their

faces grimy, their hair matted with mud. The colour of
Suzanne's brown handbag had run and had left large brown
stains all over her raincoat. The couple spent an hour restoring
some kind of decency to their appearance, and Suzanne added
a finishing touch by putting ribbons in her hair. Then they
made their way to the nearest station, and safely reached Tours
and Paris. But it had been a close call.

*   *   *

Sometimes Paul would go up north on missions, and Suzanne
would spend some days on her own in Paris, filling in the time
finding new safe houses in which to put the escaping British
soldiers overnight, and distributing resistance publications.
Whenever a new batch of soldiers was due in Paris she nearly
always received an enigmatically-worded letter from the Abbé
Carpentier in Lille, so that she was able to make preparations
for their reception. Thus on October 30, 1941, the Abbé sent
her a letter which read, in part:—

"Paul came through here yesterday with his whole team
of footballers (fifteen in all including the 'supporters'). As
they all talked at the same time, we were not able to exchange
any very serious information. They were very gay and counted
greatly on their speed and their team spirit to win this new
match."

Paul and his party were obviously in good heart, but later in
the Abbé's letter there was a slightly ominous note. For he told
Suzanne, in carefully chosen words:—

"One of my cousins was recently very alarmed. Her
neighbour Madame Deram was disturbed by the Gestapo,
nobody knows why . . . I wonder what is going on in the
north? . . . for there have been several consecutive arrests or
mysterious departures. . . . I send you my most paternal
benediction and my greetings."

This was the first hint that had come to Suzanne from anybody that the Germans might be on the track of the escape organisation. But Suzanne, reading the Abbé's letter, paid no great attention to his faint expression of uneasiness, and prepared to welcome Paul and his party of "footballers" on their passage through Paris. And when she met them at the Gare du Nord a couple of days later, Paul was his usual cheerful self. Suzanne accompanied this party south and also another party of three. On one of her trips her footballers included a young American named Oscar, blond, with blue eyes, who had volunteered for service with the R.A.F. even though America was not yet in the war. Suzanne could hardly believe he was really a pilot, for he looked so fresh and young. The train was bitterly cold and when she drew off her heavy army boots to rub her freezing feet, the young American said, "Pardon me, Miss" and rubbed her feet tenderly for her. Later she learned from official records that the young American had been Pilot Officer Oscar Coen, who was born in North Dakota but whose home was in Chicago, Illinois. Coen had crashed south of Hazebrouck, France, on October 20, 1941. Almost at once he had contacted and had been taken in charge by the escape organisation. (He is now a distinguished officer in the U.S.A.A.F.). Suzanne located him in 1958 with the help of an American newspaper.

The party conducted south on this particular trip was the largest single party of men whom Suzanne had helped on their way to freedom all in a single group. It consisted of no fewer than fifteen men. Suzanne, of course, never knew all their names, but official records at the Air Ministry were able, years after the war, to tell her the names of most of the men whom she had aided on this occasion. They included Squadron Leader H. E. Bufton (now Group Captain Bufton, D.S.O., O.B.E., D.F.C., A.F.C.), Flight Lieutenant R. G. A. Barclay, D.F.C. (killed in action on July 17, 1942), Sergeants Bell, Read and Crampton of the R.A.F., and eight army other ranks.

When, about ten days later, Paul took another party south he told Suzanne: "No need for you to come on this trip, Suzie," and he gave her instead some task to do for him in Paris. Clearly he had some reason of his own for not wanting her with him on this occasion, and she did not question him.

So, while Paul journeyed south again to Marseilles, Suzanne remained behind in Tante Jeanne's flat. Paul was away about a week, and when he returned to Paris he seemed to Suzanne strangely upset.

"There was a spot of bother down in Marseilles this time," he told her. "I had a bit of a row with somebody and had to tell them where they got off."

"Why, what happened?" asked Suzanne.

"Oh its nothing to worry about, really," said Paul airily. "I can't stop now to tell you about it, I've got important things to do up north. Don't worry, Suzie. You know you can trust me, don't you?" And the same day he left Paris again for Lille.

Suzanne was not unduly disturbed. She felt confident that if there were any real trouble Paul was the man who would always be able to iron it out.

*   *   *

"You know you can trust me."

The phrase ran like a recurring theme through the encounters of Suzanne with her new-found hero. It was reassurance, calming every fear, sweeping away every misgiving. The British Army, "the Regiment", Scotland Yard, the misty prestige of the "Intelligence Service"—they were the glamorous background to Paul's personality—and his present feats and positive achievements were enough to prove their worth.

So it was with trust and satisfaction that, in the second week of December, Suzanne, waiting in Paris, heard news of Cole again. She received a message from him instructing her to meet him once more at the Gare du Nord with another team of "footballers".

And thus Suzanne was at the Gare du Nord on the morning of December 11, stamping her feet on the cold, misty platform, walking up and down and awaiting the arrival of the train from Lille. But before the train arrived, Vladimir de Fliguë turned up, and hurried to Suzanne with a message.

"Don't wait for the train, Suzanne," said he. "Cole is not coming in on it."

"Why, what has happened?" asked Suzanne, a little anxiously, suddenly remembering the hints that Paul had dropped about trouble in the organisation.

"There's been a little difficulty up north," replied de Fliguë. I've just heard from Cole, and he's been delayed for a few days."

By the next morning Suzanne still had received no further message from Cole and was becoming increasingly anxious. She decided to see de Fliguë once again and went down to his little factory, where the electrical resistances were made, just across the street from his home. There she found his wife in tears.

"Suzanne, get out," said Madame de Fliguë, "and get out quickly. My husband was arrested here yesterday along with Professor Holweck—and Paul Cole."

The news came as a deep shock to Suzanne. So not only had Paul been arrested but he had also been in Paris without letting her know. Why had he made de Fliguë lie to her in sending her a message to the station saying that he was not in town?

"But I though Paul was still in the North?" Suzanne asked Madame de Fliguë.

"No. In fact he came here yesterday, but he asked my husband not to tell you or anybody else that he was in Paris."

"Whatever for?"

"I've no idea."

Suzanne hurried out of the factory into the street. From the shelter of a doorway, a man in a long dark overcoat stepped out a few yards behind her. Suzanne saw him, quickened her steps and quickly turned the corner of the street towards the Métro station of Monge. She was being followed. She was convinced of it. The Germans who had arrested Paul were waiting to take her, too.

When she got into the train at the Monge station she was frightened to see that the man entered the same train. As one station after another went by, Suzanne's brain was working rapidly. First, trouble in the north, and now the three arrests in Paris. There must be somewhere a traitor denouncing everybody, denouncing even Paul. At all costs she must shake off the man who seemed to be following her, and get away down to Marseilles.

Suzanne used the classic trick recommended to all agents who are being followed. She waited in the train until the moment before it was due to leave a station. Then, just as the doors were closing, she hopped out on to the platform—and saw the train disappearing into the tunnel, with the man staring angrily after her. Changing trains twice more as a precaution, she finally reached the flat of Tante Jeanne and quickly began to pack a few things together into a little handbag, only a few things, because she would have to carry the bag herself on the all-night walk through the fields across the demarcation line. She planned to catch the train that very afternoon to Tours and, if all went well, to cross the border that same night.

But gradually, as she was packing, Suzanne grew a little calmer. Suddenly she remembered Durand and her friends at the Chope du Pont Neuf and thought, "I must warn them, if they haven't already been arrested too." She left her packing and went straight out to the telephone booth at the Becon-les-Bruyères station to telephone to Durand.

Even on the telephone in occupied Paris you had to be careful what you said. So when Durand came on the line Suzanne told him in guarded tones, "Monsieur Durand this is just to let you know that Paul is very sick—he has had an accident and has been taken away to hospital. I'm afraid it's something very dangerous and I thought you ought to know." But her warning went unheeded.

"Oh no, Suzanne," said Durand in a surprised voice. "I'm sure you are mistaken. Why, Paul phoned me himself only an hour or so ago."

"Then it can't really have been Paul speaking to you," protested Suzanne. "I *know* he's in hospital, and very sick too."

"But it was," insisted Durand. "I'd know Paul's voice anywhere. He's coming to the restaurant at three o'clock tomorrow afternoon. Why don't you come too and have a beer with us?"

More puzzled than ever, Suzanne hung up and returned to her aunt's flat. Was Paul arrested or was he free? What was really happening? In any case she decided to delay her own flight and go to the restaurant next afternoon in the hope of seeing Paul. It was a fateful decision. Looking back afterwards, Suzanne realised that if only she had not stopped to telephone Durand and had gone straight on her way south, she would have been spared all the drama which followed.

But next afternoon at three o'clock she went to the Chope du Pont Neuf and sat there with the grave and sympathetic Durand on the red banquette, sipping a weak beer and waiting for Cole.

And suddenly Paul walked in—not accompanied, clearly not arrested, seemingly in good spirits though in a state of high excitement.

"Why, Paul," said Suzanne, "I heard you'd been arrested—whatever happened to you?"

"Suzanne, my dear," said Paul, "I've had the biggest bit of luck in the world. I've been arrested and then I escaped. I simply must tell you both all about it."

Together the three sat down at one of the marble-topped tables at the rear of the restaurant, and Paul went on; "You know, de Fliguë, Holweck and I—we've all just had the most wonderful escape."

Suzanne's eyes filled with admiration as she listened to Cole's account of events, told with great conviction and the almost professional sense of drama which he always displayed when he had a story to tell. To the young French girl it seemed that once more "Pimpernel Paul" had proved that he could meet any situation.

"What happened was this," said Cole excitedly. "I was just going into the street with de Fliguë and the Professor, when suddenly we saw the Germans there waiting for us. They drew their guns, and I had a fight with one of them, but they finally got us all three into their car, and drove off towards their head-quarters. There we were in the car, all of us handcuffed, of course, and sitting together in the back seat of the car, with one German policeman and a driver in front. It was that which gave us our chance.

"Well, you know what a big strong man Professor Holweck is, even if he is nearly sixty. So I whispered a plan to the other two. Suddenly the professor leaned foward and threw his hand-cuffed hands over the head and tightly round the neck of the policeman, nearly strangling him, while I did the same thing with the chap who was driving the car. We forced them into a side street and made them stop. Then we all three jumped out and just ran like hell. The two Germans drew their guns and followed us with a real fusillade of bullets—but we made it. Now de Fliguë and the professor and I are safely in hiding in a house of some friends of the professor. That's where you come in, Suzanne. I want you to help me get them away across the border and into the free zone. We've simply got to help those two chaps, eh?"

"Oh yes," said Suzanne enthusiastically. "What is it you want me to do, Paul?"

"Get them clothes and a new set of identity cards," said Paul.

"Of course," agreed Suzanne promptly. "I can get the clothes this afternoon and take them myself to the place where they are hidden. It's safer for me to go there than for you to go back again."

Paul hesitated a moment—and his hesitation faintly puzzled Suzanne. "Well, er—no, actually Suzanne I think it's better you don't go there yourself. Tell you what; you get the clothes and bring them here to the restaurant and leave them in the cloak-room. Then I'll come in the evening and pick them up."

"But why can't I go with them myself?" asked Suzanne, a little hurt. "Is it that you don't trust me to get the clothes to them safely?"

"Of course not, silly girl," said Paul, and he went on quickly, "it's just that I think my way is the best. It's too dangerous a job for you. And also the people who are hiding them are very scared and I've given them my word of honour that I won't tell a soul where they are, and that nobody shall go there but me."

So a little reluctantly Suzanne agreed, and Paul told her cheerfully, "Well, I must be on my way now. Got a lot to do. But I'll be back here tomorrow evening and pick up the clothes."

Suzanne telephoned to a woman friend and in careful language explained what had happened. The woman agreed to bring around some clothes for the two men the next afternoon. And when she turned up at the restaurant she was delighted to hear Suzanne's account, as given to her by Paul, of how the three men had escaped.

"Are you really sure they are all safe?" asked the woman.

"Well I haven't seen the other two, but I've seen Paul," said Suzanne. "And obviously if he is safe the others must be too."

"Oh, how splendid," said the woman. "That Paul, he's a bright one, isn't he?" And Suzanne agreed that he was.

Suzanne stayed on at the Chope du Pont Neuf all next afternoon, dallying over a beer and waiting for Paul to come back and collect the clothes.

Finally, just after darkness had fallen, the glass door of the brasserie was burst open with a clatter and Paul, looking breathless and dishevelled, dashed in.

"Quick, Suzanne, get out of here," he cried. "The Gestapo are after us. Get to the corner of the street and wait for me there."

Without hesitating for any explanation, Suzanne did as she was told. She ran down the street in the black-out and waited at a dark corner, by a shuttered shop. Paul joined her a moment later, and as he did so, Suzanne heard the screech of brakes of a black Citroen saloon—the cars used mainly by the German police in France—jerking to a stop outside the brasserie.

"Quick, this way," urged Paul, and the couple darted round a corner, down a street and disappeared quickly into the entrance to the Pont Neuf Métro station.

"Phew!" exclaimed Paul, mopping his brow as they sank on to a seat of the underground train, "that was a really narrow squeak."

Talking in low tones together as the underground train rattled through the tunnel, Paul and Suzanne considered what to do next, as it was essential that Paul should find a new hiding place.

"I know a woman who runs a clinic in Paris," said Paul. "She might let me hide out there, at least for tonight."

So the couple changed trains and headed for the clinic. But on the way they ran into still more trouble.

For at the great underground junction which is now called Franklin D. Roosevelt (and in those days was named the Rond Point des Champs Elysées), they ran smack into a police control. The French policemen had stationed themselves cleverly just around a corner of one of the long tunnels which lead from one platform to another, so that they could not be seen from a distance, and by the time Paul and Suzanne had encountered them, it was too late to turn back.

"Your papers, please," said one of the three *agents* operating the control.

For a moment Suzanne wondered what to do. Her own papers were, of course, perfectly in order as a French girl working in Paris, and she would have no difficulty in passing the control. But Paul had no papers at all. There was nothing to prevent Suzanne just showing her identity card and walking past the policeman, pretending that she had nothing to do with Paul, and leaving him behind to his fate. But she could not abandon Paul Cole in his new moment of danger. So she stopped by his side as he hesitated in front of the policeman, felt in all his pockets, and finally said, in an accent which was all too unmistakably English, "Je regrette mais jay oubliay mon portefeuille."

The policeman looked at Paul somewhat quizzically and replied, "Well, monsieur, if you have forgotten your papers, I'm sorry but I am afraid you will have to come with me to the police station." But the policeman said it very quietly and he didn't start shouting for his colleagues or accuse Paul directly of being an Englishman, and this gave Suzanne a sudden hope that they still had a chance of getting by.

So Suzanne, quick-witted as usual, began talking to the policeman—and talking fast. She told him a long and obviously imaginary story about how Paul was her fiancé who had just been released from a German prisoner-of-war camp and therefore had no papers and that they were just going out together for the evening, until suddenly the policeman interrupted her. "Well, I'll let you pass this once," he said, "But don't go around in Paris without papers—it's liable to get you into a whole lot of trouble." And with what seemed to Suzanne the trace of a knowing wink, the good French policeman let them pass. He obviously believed that Paul was an escaping British pilot— and, despite his orders imposed on the French police by the Germans, he knew where his own sympathies lay.

All the time Suzanne was talking to the policeman she had felt perfectly calm and self-possessed. But, as she and Paul later climbed the staircase of the Métro to their platform, she confessed to Paul, "My legs feel just like jelly."

Finally they got to the clinic—but no good fortune met them

there. The woman in charge refused to take Paul in when she heard that he was being actively hunted by the Germans. "I didn't mind putting you up when you were just passing through Paris," she told Paul, "but not this time—it's too dangerous, and there are too many people in this clinic whom I can't trust."

Reluctantly Paul and Suzanne turned away from the door. Standing in the cold and dark garden on that December night they debated what to do next.

"Can't you find me somewhere to go—just for tonight at any rate?" asked Paul.

Quickly Suzanne tried to think out what was the right course for her to take. If she let Paul accompany her back to Tante Jeanne's flat, she ran the risk of putting her elderly aunt into great peril. The Germans had arrested older people than Tante Jeanne and sent them to concentration camps for offences not so great as sheltering an escaping Englishman. Yet how could she refuse a refuge to a man who had done so much good work?

Finally she took her decision. "You can come home with me to Tante Jeanne, Paul," she said. "But I must tell her the truth about you this time and she must decide for herself whether she will take you in."

By now it was getting late and they hurried to catch their train to Becon-les-Bruyères. When a sleepy Tante Jeanne greeted them in her flat Suzanne told her at once, "Look, Tante Jeanne, this man Paul Cole isn't an American journalist, as I told you before, but he's an Englishman and he's wanted by the German police, and he has no money, no papers and desperately needs somewhere to sleep. What do you think we ought to do about him?"

"Why, let him stay here, of course," said Tante Jeanne, who had not earned her membership of the Three Musketeers for nothing.

"But you realise the danger, Tante Jeanne?"

"Hurry up, Suzanne, and give the man something hot to eat. Monsieur looks starving." Thankfully Paul Cole dossed down in a sofa in Tante Jeanne's flat that night.

Across the other side of Paris just then, at the Chope du Pont Neuf restaurant, the Germans were arresting M. Durand and his two waiters and taking them to Lille for interrogation. All three were beaten up and asked, time and again, "Where is Paul Cole?" Finally they were released for lack of evidence.

But, in Tante Jeanne's flat in Paris, twenty-four hours after the arrival of Cole, a totally unexpected problem presented itself to Suzanne and her hospitable aunt. And this was one which had nothing to do with the German police.

For Paul suddenly fell sick with a raging fever. It happened so quickly there was no time to talk about it, no time for Paul to give Suzanne and her aunt any explanation. Suddenly, next afternoon, they found him lying on a bed, his brow perspiring and red-hot, and completely delirious. He could take no food, but avidly gulped down water. He was so weak that he could not move from the bed. With growing anxiety the two women debated what to do. They dared not call a doctor and thereby reveal the presence in their flat of an Englishman wanted by the Germans. They could only nurse him themselves, and hope for the best. Almost hourly they had to change the sheets on his bed, which were soaking wet from perspiration. Tante Jeanne still had some aspirin left in her bathroom cupboard and they forced some tablets down Paul Cole's throat.

But still his fever mounted and his delirious babbling became more frantic than ever. He seemed to be growing steadily weaker and could now hardly lift his head to drink a glass of water. A new anxiety gripped the two women watching anxiously at his bedside. What if Paul Cole should die, right there, in Tante Jeanne's flat? What in the world would they do with the body?

Suzanne and her aunt went into the little salon and sat down together at the inlaid antique table to discuss this new and macabre problem. It was, in its grim way, like a scene from *Arsenic and Old Lace*, with the small, frail and dignified Tante Jeanne debating with Suzanne how far from the house she and Suzanne would be able to carry Cole's body if he died.

"We would have to take it a long way away," pointed out Suzanne practically, "because Paul has been seen coming here several times before and if his body was found anywhere near this street people would know that he belonged to us."

"We would have to do it in the middle of the night," said Tante Jeanne doubtfully.

And then a new thought struck them. The stairs leading up to Tante Jeanne's flat were narrow and winding. It would be extremely hard for the little elderly Frenchwoman and the twenty-year-old Suzanne to carry the six-foot body of Paul down the two stories. "And, in any case," said Tante Jeanne, "we must get him down, if he dies, very quickly, before his body goes — stiff. Otherwise we could never get him round the corners."

"Oh how dreadful this is, Tante Jeanne," shuddered Suzanne.

So the women went back and inspected Paul, and to their surprise and relief they thought he seemed a little better. All that night they continued giving him cold compresses, aspirin and glasses of water. Finally Cole fell into a deep sleep—and when he awoke his fever had gone, as suddenly as it had appeared.

Cole lay weakly in the bed and smiled somewhat sheepishly at Suzanne and Tante Jeanne.

"Sorry to have given you both such a lot of trouble, ladies," he said. "Must have been a touch of malaria. Got it during my service with the Indian Army."

With skill and devotion Suzanne and the elderly Frenchwoman nursed Paul Cole back to health. Tante Jeanne spent what little money she could afford on buying the invalid delicacies on the black market—a little extra butter, sometimes an egg.

Daily Suzanne sat with Paul Cole and talked, and listened to his seemingly inexhaustible fund of stories of his past adventures and exploits. She was impressed by what he told her. It is probably quite normal that she should have failed to notice that Cole was a "public school type" who never mentioned his public school, a "regimental officer" who never talked about his regiment. To Suzanne, at this time, Paul was quite simply a British hero in need of shelter and help, and a man whose personal attractions she was beginning increasingly to appreciate. Besides, the adventures which the two of them had already shared would in themselves have been enough to have drawn them naturally together.

* * *

Gradually, under the vigilant ministrations of Tante Jeanne, Paul Cole recovered his strength and his customary confidence. His gentle, courteous manner, his readiness to help around the apartment—he was always able with his hands, the kind of man who fixes a leaking tap or a broken fuse in a moment—won the heart of Suzanne's aunt. He fixed her geyser and repaired her shoes. And in the evenings he would charm her by singing to her in his soft and attractive voice the current English hit-tune, "Little Old Lady Passing By".

"Vraiment il est très gentil," declared Tante Jeanne to Suzanne, and the young girl confided, "Auntie, I think he's marvellous. After de Gaulle, I admire him more than anybody. Think of going around in France and doing all he has done despite that broad English accent. How brave he must be."

When Christmas came Tante Jeanne and Suzanne scraped up every franc they could afford to lay on a special dinner for their Englishman.

It took Paul Cole a week or more to recover from his bout of malaria. And it was while he was still convalescent that an odd little incident occurred which might, if only Suzanne had read the signs correctly, have given her some warning of a weakness in Paul's make-up.

Because he had no clothes of his own, Suzanne had borrowed pyjamas for him from her cousin, Charles Warenghem, who lived not far away. But the December weather was bitterly cold and the apartment, like others in Paris at that time, had little heating. One morning when Suzanne carried in breakfast in bed to Paul, she found him shivering. "I'll get you something to wrap yourself up in," she promised him.

Suzanne had an old red sweater on which she had pinned a brooch which had been given to her as a memento by one of the British soldiers whom she had helped to escape. It was only an ordinary lieutenant's pip round which had been stuck three rows of little glass beads in red, white and blue respectively. It was a thing of no monetary—and no great artistic—value, but Suzanne treasured it because of the exploit of which it reminded her. She put the old red sweater with the brooch over Paul's back, and thought no more about it.

But next day, when she wanted to wear the red sweater herself, she found that the brooch was missing. She supposed that Paul had taken it out because it was sticking into his back, and she innocently asked him, "I say, where's the brooch that was on this sweater?"

"I never saw any brooch on it," said Paul.

"Well, it was on yesterday when I put the sweater on you," said Suzanne.

"You must be wrong, Suzie," argued Paul. "I would have noticed it if it had been there."

For days Suzanne searched the flat for the missing brooch and later, when he was able to get up, Paul helped her look for it too. But the brooch was never found and, in the light of all that happened afterwards, Suzanne finally came to realise that Paul himself had quietly pocketed it—probably to give as a "regimental" memento to one of his girl friends.

During Cole's convalescence, Suzanne began to ply him with

questions about what exactly had happened up in the north and how his own arrest had come about. They were detailed and penetrating questions, but Cole always had an answer to them.

"There were a whole series of arrests in the North," he told her, "just before I came down to Paris. It was pretty serious. They even got the Abbé Carpentier too."

Suzanne pondered. She finally said: "Then, Paul, the only explanation is that somebody must have been giving things away to the Germans—there must have been a traitor."

"That's it," said Paul. "I'm sure there must have been a traitor, and what's more I think I know who it was."

"Who do you mean?"

"I'm pretty sure it must have been Roland Lepers; after all he was the only chap except myself who knew all the addresses. Poor Roland must have been caught and then denounced everybody. I never thought he would have done a thing like that."

The suggestion seemed a shocking one to Suzanne, who had worked with Lepers and knew him as a brave patriot, devoted to the cause.

In the weeks that followed Christmas and as Paul regained his strength, Suzanne suggested that she ought to make a trip south, to renew contact with the organisation in Marseilles. But Paul objected: "No, it's not wise for you to do that, Suzie. Whoever the traitor was, he probably knew the names of everybody in the south; no doubt he's denounced them all to the Vichy police by now."

A better way, argued Cole, would be for Suzanne to get him a new set of identity papers so that he himself could go again to the north of France and try to rebuild the organisation. "There are a few people up there whom Lepers didn't know," said Paul. "I must try to get into touch with them."

"Why don't you let me go up north, then, instead of you?" volunteered Suzanne. "My papers are in order, and it would be much safer for me to travel there than for you to be seen in that area again."

But Cole was having none of this, either.

"No," he said, "That would never do. With all the trouble there has been up north, nobody would trust you, because they've never seen you before. Believe me, it's much better for you to get me some new identity cards and let me take a trip."

So, while Cole remained hidden in Tante Jeanne's flat right through January and most of February, Suzanne procured for him from her friends the Crépels a set of new, false but very convincing-looking identity papers. Finally, at the beginning of March 1942, Paul set off on his mysterious mission to the north.

In the weeks which followed Cole made several trips between Paris and the north, using Tante Jeanne's flat as his Paris base. He never told Suzanne where he went nor whom he visited, but Suzanne saw nothing at all strange in this secrecy. It was a perfectly normal practice in the Resistance that each member should know only what was strictly necessary for his own particular work so that, if captured and tortured by the Gestapo, the agent could reveal only a limited amount of information.

Suzanne was glad to see Paul restored to health and apparently his own active self again. And with every visit which he paid to Tante Jeanne's flat, Suzanne felt her own personal ties with Paul becoming closer and more intimate. There was no doubt about it, something like genuine love was springing up between the two, and this was almost inevitable after nearly half a year of close association, of adventures, dangers and hardships shared, and with the additional impulse of Suzanne's romantic admiration for the work that Paul Cole was doing. Suzanne was obviously becoming increasingly eager to link her fate to Paul's. Yet now there was a second vaguely sinister incident which this time did cause a faint shadow of a doubt to fall across her mind. It happened just after Paul Cole had returned from one of his journeys.

As he sat down at supper with Tante Jeanne and Suzanne

that evening, Cole said, with a touch of pride in his voice, "I'm a real 'Wanted Man' these days up in the north. The Germans are looking for me everywhere. Why, they've even stuck my picture up all over the place, are printing it in the papers and are offering a big reward for my recapture. Look, I brought back one of the photographs they're circulating of me, as a souvenir."

And, dragging a cutting of paper from his pocket, Paul showed the two women a printed picture of a man who did indeed appear to be himself. It was a photograph which showed mainly a back view of the man, with only a small portion of the face visible. The man was wearing a raincoat and a soft felt hat, both of the type that Paul always wore. He seemed to be standing too, in an attitude that was characteristic of Paul Cole, so that the two admiring women did not doubt for a moment that the picture was actually of him.

"Oh, Paul," said Suzanne, "you really must be careful what you do now."

Next morning Suzanne had an appointment at her dentist's and was spending the usual period in the waiting-room idly running through the ancient illustrated papers on his table. By chance her eye caught sight of a picture which made her sit up with a sharp exclamation of dismay. The photograph bore the legend, "Dr. ——— entering his famous clinic in Geneva." And it was precisely the same picture which Cole had produced from his pocket the previous evening. Obviously he had found a copy of the same paper somewhere in northern France, had noticed the resemblance of the photograph to himself, and had torn out the picture with the sole idea of impressing Suzanne and her aunt. Furious, Suzanne abandoned her dentist's appointment, tore the incriminating page from the illustrated paper and rushed home. Paul was sitting there before lunch entertaining Tante Jeanne and her cousin Charles with his repertoire of anecdotes. Waving the paper in front of his eyes, Suzanne delivered herself of a furious onslaught.

"What's the idea of lying to me like this," she asked him. "What are you doing, trying to show off? Do you think I need to be impressed in this sort of silly way."

Cole put up a show of enormous surprise and injured pride.

"I was given that picture by a member of the Resistance in the north who told me it was my photograph," he declared. "How could I know that it was not. And how dare you, a silly little girl like you, doubt the word and good-will of a British officer?"

It was the first really serious quarrel which Suzanne had had with Paul Cole, but her pride had been hurt by what she considered his stupid trick and she flounced off into her bedroom and slammed and locked the door. Cole knocked on the door several times, and called through it, "Suzanne, Suzanne, how could you think I would play such a game with you?" But Suzanne refused to speak to him any more for the rest of that day. And that evening she found that Cole had gone out leaving a note for her behind him. The note, obviously written with righteous indignation, read, in part:—

"Suzy darling,

I see *plainly* that you do not wish to understand my state of mind at this awful moment. Why do you wish to always misunderstand things?

Place yourself in my position and I am sure you will see more clearly.

Please understand that you called me a liar in front of your cousin this morning without knowing what had been said. I can not permit this. My first thought is always of you, your safety, happiness and love. When! oh when!! will you understand this.

However, as you always think the worst, and as I do not wish to quarrel with you, I will leave immediately I get papers for the North of France. . . . I will not rest to see you unhappy or perhaps lose your esteem."

Paul had signed the letter with his initials, with two small crosses representing kisses, and had added a post-script; "I write this because you will not speak to me."

Faced with this challenge, Suzanne's defences gave way. When Paul came back to her aunt's flat again, she told him, "I'm sorry, too, that it happened—it's only that I admired you so much it just wasn't necessary for you to do anything to make me admire you even more. And when I am so frightened for your safety you ought not to make me more frightened still." And Cole offered her an embrace which was only partly paternal.

That was their first, but it was not their only quarrel. Obviously it was a strain for a young girl like Suzanne to be thrown in close proximity with an active man, a typically handsome British officer, and the strain of knowing that there was always the danger of discovery and arrest by the German police added to the tense atmosphere in Tante Jeanne's little flat. But whenever there was trouble with Suzanne, Paul Cole seemed always to know just how to put things right again, sometimes with a protestation of his genuine love for her and sometimes with a touch of fatherly advice—"You are so young, my dear, and you must understand that I know best." After one of their minor disputes, Cole went out from Tante Jeanne's flat early the following morning, leaving behind him another characteristic note for Suzanne. It read:—

"Little Girl,

This morning I understand how difficult I am to get along with. Perhaps I am too old, perhaps worried, I do not know! Please, dearest, do not pity me. Should you find me unbearable, well just let me drift along alone. . . . If I hurt you sometimes I am sorry."

And this time Cole signed the note with the initials "H.C." and added the title of rank in the Royal Engineers which he customarily used; "Lieut. R.E."

Once again, after receiving this appeal, Suzanne agreed to make up the lovers' quarrel. But it was obvious that the personal relations between herself and Cole would have to come to a crisis-point before very long. It came sooner than she expected. For one day Paul Cole suddenly but decisively proposed; "Suzie, we must get married."

"But how can we do it?" she asked him wonderingly. "The German police have certainly given your name to the French by now. They will be on the look-out for you everywhere. You can't get married in your own name—and if you marry me in a false one, it won't be a real marriage at all."

"We must do it by hook or by crook," said Paul with a smile. "Let's ask the advice of Tante Jeanne."

Suzanne's good aunt, of course, was thrilled by the news, as were Tante Marie and Tante Isabelle to whom the secret was also confided. "It's a proper English gentleman whom our Suzanne is marrying," they all agreed. And Paul smiled a slightly enigmatic smile.

The former Vicar of the church at Becon-les-Bruyères where Suzanne had been baptised was the round, red-faced and genial Abbé Amy, a close personal friend of Tante Isabelle, and a man whom everbody knew they could trust. Just now he was officiating at the church of Notre Dame de la Medaille Miraculeuse, in the outlying suburb of Malakoff. So Tante Isabelle was dispatched to Malakoff to talk the matter over with the Abbé. He promptly agreed to help.

Years later, when I saw the Abbé (he is to-day Canon of the great church of Notre Dame de Vincennes), he told me; "Mademoiselle Bureau told me that Suzanne wanted to marry one of the Chiefs of the British Intelligence Service who was living secretly in Paris. Since I was in the Resistance myself and because I had known Suzanne from the time she was a little girl, I could not possibly refuse. But there were, of course, several serious difficulties in the way."

First Paul Cole himself was sent off to have an interview

with Abbé Amy. The Abbé explained to him that, since Cole himself was a Protestant and Suzanne a Catholic, he must first obtain in the normal way the authorisation of the Archbishop of Paris before he could carry out any church ceremony. But this, he believed, could be arranged—as, indeed, it was.

More serious was the fact that in France a priest is not allowed by law to carry out a religious marriage before the couple have produced to him a certificate that they have been through the form of civil marriage in some official town hall.

As the Abbé Amy later related to me: "Paul listened to my explanation with great care, and finally assured me that he could obtain the certificate, which I needed for my own protection. He finished up by telling me stories about his activities as a British Intelligence agent in France and told them so convincingly that I believed every word he said. He struck me as a man of extreme psychological force, very agreeable, very attractive."

So, having charmed the Abbé as he had charmed so many other people, Paul Cole set to work to secure the necessary paper certifying that he and Suzanne had already been through the form of civil marriage which the French law required. And later he handed to the priest a certificate that he and Suzanne had been married by the Mayor of some town hall in the Pas de Calais area. It was, of course, a forgery, designed to protect the Abbé from possible trouble with the French authorities.

Thus everything was finally prepared for what must surely have been one of the strangest weddings to take place throughout the last war, the bride a young, trusting and courageous resistance worker; the bridegroom an Englishman already known to be on the run from the Gestapo.

It was a fine, sunny Spring day as the odd little party gathered in the shabby, unpretentious church of Notre Dame, set back a little from the other buildings in the busy shopping street, the Avenue Pierre Larousse, and half-hidden by the grocer's shop which stands next to it. Inside, the church looked a little more impressive, with the cold bright sunlight shining through the stained glass windows on to the pale blue statue of the Virgin with arms outstretched above the gilt altar. Candles were burning in the church, and above the altar as he entered no doubt Paul Cole read the inscription "O Marie, Forgive us our sins and pray for those of us who turn to you."

Because Paul was a Protestant, the wedding ceremony was carried out in the sacristry, and nobody was present except the bridal couple, the Abbé in his long cassock, and Suzanne's aunts. Paul, his fair hair neatly brushed, appeared a highly respectable bridegroom in a well-pressed grey suit and light tie. Suzanne, her round young face flushed with happiness, looked positively radiant in a dress of beige and pink, a new navy blue summer coat and a navy blue hat framing her dark curls.

The Abbé Amy had arranged to keep the ceremony down to its bare essentials, to eliminate the customary mass, and to have no organist present. And, as an extra measure of prudence, he had not even mentioned to his sacristan that there was anything particularly unusual about this little, unobtrusive war-time wedding.

For a few moments the couple knelt side-by-side in silent prayer. Then they rose to their feet and the Abbé turned to Cole.

"Will you take Suzanne here present as your legitimate wife according to the rites of our Mother the Holy Church."

"Je le veux," replied Cole in the best French he could manage.

"Do you promise to guard her faithfully in all things like a faithful husband should his wife, according to the commandment of God?"

"Yes."

"And what do you give her?"

In a firm and completely assured voice Cole gave the ritual answer, "My Faith."

And the aunts, standing in their Sunday-best clothes in the

background were greatly moved as they watched the slim figure of Suzanne turn towards Cole to receive her wedding-ring, and the kindly-faced Abbé enveloped the couple in his stole as he pronounced the final Latin words, "Ego conjungo vos in matrimonium, in nomine Patris et Filii et Spiritus Sancti. Amen."

The Abbé's address was kept brief and in very general terms and at its conclusion the couple moved over to sign their names in the Church Registry book. Under the section for personal details, Cole wrote in a firm, neat hand:—

> Name: Cole, Harold.
> Born: Marquette par Lille.
> January 24, 1903.
> Son of: Albert Thomas,
> Alice Anne Godfrey.

He appended his correct signature, "Harold Cole," bestowed a kiss on Suzanne and then offered her his arm to escort her from the church.

A little wedding breakfast was held in a restaurant, where they were joined by a friend of Cole, Julien de la Tour, who was a head waiter at a café on the Boulevard St. Michel and who had helped him in his early Resistance work, and also Julien's wife, who brought along a carved ivory powder-box as a wedding present. And in the evening Tante Jeanne threw a small wedding reception in her flat at Becon-les-Bruyères. There were fewer than a dozen people there—Suzanne and Paul, the aunts, Suzanne's friends, Jeanne and Francine Crépel, and her cousin Charles with his small son. Tante Jeanne had filled the flat with flowers and somehow, despite rationing which was becoming severe by 1942, had managed to collect a quantity of good food, while the Crepéls produced some champagne which they had been keeping hidden to celebrate Victory Day. It was a gay and care-free evening. Everyone said that Suzanne had never looked prettier and Paul, at the top of his form, gave once more his celebrated rendering of "Little Old Lady". Recalling that evening years afterwards, Francine Crépel told me, "Paul was a real charmer". And it was obvious that Suzanne thought so too.

Certainly nobody in the gay gathering that night suspected even for one moment the real nature of the bridegroom's character. But the truth was that Paul Cole, the man to whom Suzanne had now linked her fate, was neither Captain nor Lieutenant in the British Army, but a Sergeant who had deserted from it, and a traitor who had already denounced a number of his friends to the Germans and who soon would be denouncing many more.

PART THREE

Trust—and Treason

PEOPLE talk about a "woman's intuition"—but never, surely, did a girl's inmost feelings deceive her more completely than in the trust which twenty-year-old Suzanne Warren had, like so many older and wiser people, placed in Paul Cole. In her case, no doubt, her confidence in him stemmed from a mixture of romantic innocence, fervent patriotism and uncritical faith. But it was calamitous. And the calamity went on. For even now, after she had married her self-assured Englishman, Suzanne still had not the slightest inkling of the betrayals which he had committed, nor of the true nature of the events which had gone before, and in which she herself had all unwittingly become involved.

The story went back to before Dunkirk when Cole, a London engineer who had joined the Royal Engineers in 1939 and had risen to the rank of Sergeant, had stayed behind in France. He had taken shelter with various French families in the north, to whom he had told fanciful stories of being a British Intelligence Captain. Then he had indeed done good work in aiding British soldiers to escape and in building and organising the network in the North with the help of Roland Lepers whom he had met by chance.

But even in that cold, anxious winter of 1941, some of Paul's activities had begun to arouse misgivings among his own colleagues in the network.

Up in the north Cole's associates, mostly people of extremely modest means had come to be more and more puzzled by his personal habits, by his love of good living and by the amounts of money which, on occasion, he seemed to have available for the indulgence of these tastes. For instance, one day, Paul came to the home of M. Duprez (as his wife related to me when I saw her many years later) and asked several time for loans of money. Madame Duprez, who for nearly a year had shown him constant hospitality, was always ready to help but it was becoming increasingly difficult.

The Galants of Roubaix, who supplied cash to every British soldier whom they sent on his way south, were faintly surprised that the English Captain, who claimed to have such high contacts with London, never suggested at any time reimbursing them for their expenditure. And (as Madame Deram told me) as early as October in Lille there was a dispute between Cole and Roland Lepers over the sum of 10,000 francs (nearly £60 in those days) which Cole claimed to have given Lepers for paying the food bills of the British soldiers at the Chope du Pont Neuf, but which Lepers declared he had never received.

Down in the south, too, a shadow, faint at first, began gradually to darken over Paul Cole's reputation. It began with a complaint from Roland Lepers, who protested to Pat O'Leary, his Belgian colleague in the network, "Why is it that I am never allowed to see Ian Garrow myself? It's always Cole who sees him; we don't even know where he lives. I could tell him lots of things he ought to know. For instance, on that last trip it was not Cole at all who brought the batch of pilots down from the north—it was me. Cole only gave me a rendezvous in Marseilles, and we handed the men over to him there—so that he could take all the credit for himself with Ian Garrow."

That was odd; but more disturbing still were the reports which began to reach Marseilles, too, now, concerning Cole's handling of the organisation's money. Ian Garrow had given Paul certain sums to be handed over to M. Duprez for the expenses of the network in the north. Great was the consternation in Marseilles when the transparently honest M. Duprez, being asked about these sums, bluntly declared, "I never received a penny from Paul Cole."

This was obviously something which had to be investigated, and as soon as possible. But before there was time for the inquiry to get fully under way a new blow struck the organisation: Ian Garrow himself was arrested. He had arranged one day to meet a French police officer whom he believed to be a trustworthy Resistance man. But news of this encounter had somehow leaked out, and when Garrow was on his way to meet the man, other police came up and arrested him in the street. Eventually he was sent to Meauzai prison, in south-west France. From there he managed to escape to England.

This left the organisation without its leader and with the double problem of who should succeed Garrow (in the upshot it was Pat O'Leary who took over) and of what should be done about Cole? A meeting was arranged in the Marseilles flat of Dr. Rodocanachi, where Cole was confronted with M. Duprez. There was a furious quarrel, though there are differing versions of what exactly took place. Finally Cole left hurriedly for the north again and, a few days later turned up in Paris to tell Suzanne his story that there had been a "spot of bother" in Marseilles. He gave her models of stamps for false identity cards with instructions to have copies ready when he came back.

After briefly seeing Suzanne, Cole went straight on up from Paris to La Madeleine, where he arrived late at night in the house in the Avenue Bernadette which was being used as a hide-out by members of the organisation. There Madame Deram heard him opening the door and coming up the stairs. Years later she told me of her conversation with Paul that night.

As he came up the stairs, Cole shouted, "It's only me. Come on down, I've got some things to tell you."

Hastily putting on a dressing-gown Madame Deram joined Paul downstairs. He showed her an injury on his hand. "I got that in a fight in Marseilles," he told her.

"Have you been in trouble over money again?" Madame Deram asked him (for she had heard of the dispute with Roland Lepers). "No, it was nothing to do with money at all," Paul answered airily. "People have been saying all sorts of untrue things about me. We had a quarrel. I knocked a gun out of Bruce Dowding's hand, and I had to knock down Duprez, too."

Madame Deram was puzzled, but at that moment said no more. And in Paris Suzanne waited unsuspectingly for the return there of Paul with another team of "footballers".

But, alas for Paul, the German Security Police had apparently got wind of his movements and were beginning an investigation into the activities of Cole and his associates. They must have waited to start their series of arrests until Paul came back North to be sure to catch him.

About the actual course of the German inquiry into the escape network of which Cole was the chief for the North little can be known unless some day the relevant German police files come to light. But the letter which Suzanne received from the Abbé Carpentier makes it clear that, as early as October, the Security Police were already on the track of Cole and his associates and had made some arrests. Really it was almost inevitable that, sooner or later, the Germans should get wind of the network. In those early days of the war people were not always particularly security-conscious and, with virtually the whole population of the northern area at that time strongly pro-British, sometimes whole villages would know where British soldiers were hiding and who was hiding them. Sooner or later somebody was bound to drop an incautious word. And to the Germans the mysterious "Capitaine Anglais", the legendary Pimpernel of the North, must have seemed indeed a tempting prize. So through those last weeks of November and at the beginning of December, the Security Police, from their headquarters in Lille, organised and watched and planned and waited for the chance to capture in one single swoop the Englishman and the leading members of his network.

Their methodical efforts bore fruit. Somehow they located the house in Lille which was being used as a refuge for members of the escape organisation. And thus it was that, on the grey and bitterly cold morning of December 6, as snow lay over the streets of Lille, the German police suddenly swooped. Years later Madame Deram told me exactly what happened on that day at the house on the Avenue Bernadette.

"It was about ten o'clock," she related, "and I heard a knock on the door. When I opened it I saw outside two men, with six more Germans behind them. They called out, 'Police Allemande—open up' and forced their way into the house."

"I had no time to warn Paul Cole. They went through all the rooms, and burst into Paul's room upstairs and I heard them ask him for his military papers. Then they began to beat him up."

Paul Cole was brought downstairs with his arms handcuffed behind him. He was dressed only in his vest and trousers, with bare feet, while one of the German police was carrying his boots and overcoat. "You see your 'Captain Cole' now, eh?" said one of the Germans to Madame Deram with a sneer.

The stove in the hall was burning and Madame Deram had tried to stuff into it a paper in Cole's handwriting which mentioned the name of M. Duprez. One of the Germans caught her and snatched the paper out of her hands. As he was led past, Cole saw what was happening and, apparently in a sudden moment of chivalry, called out, "That paper—it's mine. It's got nothing to do with her at all." Those were the last words that Madame Deram ever heard Cole speak, for a moment later he was dragged out barefooted into the snow and pushed into one of the waiting German cars, while a policeman held Madame Deram covered with a gun. When Cole had gone, the Germans stripped Madame Deram naked and searched all her clothing for hidden papers, but they found nothing more. Finally they took her away in a second car to prison.

That same day they swooped on about ten members of the

organisation in different parts of northern France. In Roubaix, Madame Galant was taken away, but her husband, warned just in time, was able to go into hiding, and finally escaped to Britain. In La Madeleine the Germans entered the Mairie and arrested M. Duprez at his desk. Roland Lepers, who happened to be in the building at the same time, just managed to slip away unseen.

But the most fateful arrest of all that day was that of Paul Cole. For, by all accounts, it was within a few days of the moment when he was led barefoot through the snow into a German car and was motored to the prison of Loos that Cole first took his decision to turn traitor. Up to that moment, whatever his previous weaknesses had been with women or loose living, or with financial troubles, no accusation of positive treachery could have been made against him. This was the moment of his downfall.

Nobody knows exactly what happened to Cole inside the prison of Loos, and probably nobody ever will. The only thing that is certain is that Cole then and there decided to begin to betray his friends. Was he threatened with death, beaten and tortured into this decision by the Abwehr officials? Was he talked into it by those more subtle arguments at which the Abwehr were so expert? Or did Cole simply and without compulsion make an abject plea for mercy, with a promise of doing immediately anything that his captors might demand? Whatever the truth may be, within two days of his arrest, Cole began co-operating, willingly or under duress, with the Germans. And as the first of all his victims he chose the indomitable Abbé Carpentier.

In the early afternoon of December 8, only two days after his own arrest, Paul Cole turned up at the Abbé's home at Abbeville, apparently as self-assured as ever. He was accompanied by five men whom he said were escapees ready to cross the demarcation line. Two of them, Cole said, were Belgian pilots, one a British soldier, one a Captain of the R.A.F. and one a Polish pilot.

The Abbé Carpentier was just beginning to prepare their false identity cards when the German police broke in.

The Abbé and the rest of the party were led off by the German police, but Paul and the so-called Polish pilot were quickly taken away from the others. Two days later the Abbé was taken to the head office of the German Field Security police in the Rue de Tanremonde at Lille. There, sitting at the desk in the full glory of a German Lieutenant's uniform, was the man whom Cole had presented as the escaping Pole. In fact he was the officer in charge of German Security, and when he saw the Abbé he taunted him on the ease with which he had been tricked.

When Madame Duprez was allowed to visit her husband in prison he whispered in her ear, "It was Paul who denounced me." And the story of how Cole had operated was pieced together by the arrested men as they met each other in the ensuing weeks at the showers and on the exercise ground of the prison of Loos.

But it was the Abbé Carpentier who, a few months later, was able to send out from his prison cell the full and detailed indictment of Paul, which was in due course made known to the War Office in London and which registered him finally, in official British eyes, as a traitor to both his country and his friends. The Abbé's message, written in pencil on pages of small-squared paper torn from a French exercise book, was smuggled out of the prison for him by a friendly guard, and it is probably one of the most ruthless and outspoken accusations ever written by a priest. In his letter the Abbé, fervent Christian though he was, makes the frank demand that, if Cole should ever be found alive by any members of the organisation, he should be executed on the spot.

"I, as a priest, would not hesitate to burn him in cold blood. . . ." the Abbé wrote. "If you let him continue to live he will only make every situation worse and remain a constant danger for you and your colleagues. A type like that does not deserve the slightest pity; he is a monster of cowardice and weakness. The sun was not created for men like that, and he ought nót to live to see the day of Victory."

Then, to his letter, the Abbé appended his formal indictment of Cole, to be used as evidence for the War Office; it ran:—

"I, the undersigned Abbé Pierre Carpentier, living at 13 place du Cimitière-Saint-Gilles, at Abbeville (Somme), lieutenant in the reserve, certify on my religious oath and on my word of honour as an officer, the correctness of the following facts:—

"I worked with Sergeant Cole, alias Paul Delobel, from the month of March 1941, until December 8, 1941, in collaboration with Roland Lepers and one John Smith, named Jean Dubois, alias Jambe-de-Bois (wooden leg).

"During these nine months I undertook the crossing of the Somme for all the people presented to me, either in convoy or individually by each of the three people mentioned above. There passed through my hands (to the nearest ten or so) about ninety pilots, thirty soldiers and around a hundred civilians who claimed to be introduced by Cole, Lepers or Smith.

"I received from Cole about the following amounts: on one occasion one thousand francs (about £5. 15. 0 at that time—G.Y.), another time five hundred francs, three times two hundred francs and once a bicycle which was sold for six hundred francs. That money was used to cover expenses and buy presents for accomplices in Abbeville.

"I declare that I was ignobly betrayed by Sergeant Cole."

After recounting the circumstances of his arrest, as already described, the Abbé continues:—

"In the course of my preliminary examination, the examining magistrate declared to me, as he had also done to Duprez, that it was Cole who had shamefully betrayed us, not only in giving us up to the Germans but also by revealing in his declarations many things which he need not have said—doing so in order to make things worse for us, so as to be certain that we should not be released and thus be in a position to catch up with him again.

"In the course of my interrogations, I was able to establish what Cole actually had revealed. He revealed some things—such as arms hidden in my home and the homes of my friends—which were known only to himself. It was Cole who gave the Germans the plan for the search of my office at Abbeville. It was he who denounced Adolphe (alias Joseph) and André Mason (Bruce Dowding's Resistance name). His declaration (to the Germans) comprised thirty typewritten pages."

And after making various other accusations against Cole, the Abbé ended his letter, one of his last communications with the outside world, with the words, inscribed in a firm hand, "Written in the prison of Loos—P. Carpentier."

The heroic Abbé was beheaded by the Germans at Dortmund, as was also Bruce Dowding. Madame Deram spent agonising months in a concentration camp. And these were only the first of Paul's good friends to whom he brought disaster.

*   *   *

Having used Cole for their swift round-up of members of his network in the North, the Germans quickly moved him down to Paris, to gather in as many victims as they could before news of his treachery could become generally known. It was only three days after the arrest of the Abbé Carpentier that Cole turned on his friends Monsieur de Fliguë and Professor Holweck and helped the Germans to arrest them too. For the real facts of what actually happened on that afternoon of December 11, when de Fliguë and the professor had been arrested, were very different from the story which Cole later told Suzanne and Durand when he met them in the Chope du Pont Neuf. I heard the true recital of events years after the war, when Monsieur de Fliguë lunched with me in a little Paris restaurant behind the Bastille. It was the story of how

Cole had repeated in Paris the trick which he had already played on the Abbé Carpentier.

Early in the morning of December 11, Cole had, related de Fliguë, suddenly turned up at his factory in the Rue Quatrefages with two men whom he introduced as British pilots. One of the men spoke perfect English and Cole told de Fliguë, "I want you to explain to him everything he needs to know about the organisation, because he's going to take over from me for a while. I have to go on a trip to Brussels."

Slightly surprised, but not yet suspicious, de Fliguë agreed. Then Paul went on; "And about Suzanne. I wonder if you can help me out, old man. I don't want to see her on this trip. She's going to be at the Gare du Nord this morning. Do be a good chap and go along and tell her that I'm not in Paris and send her off home."

Again slightly surprised, the amiable de Fliguë agreed to do as Paul requested. Looking back on this incident as we talked, he said to me, "I'm convinced that in trying to send Suzanne away that morning Cole was making an effort to save her from getting involved in all the trouble which was falling around his own head."

And, strangely, there does seem to have been an odd streak of chivalry towards women in the make-up of the man who otherwise was a traitor. All through my inquiry I found people who spoke words of extenuation on Cole's behalf. Madame Deram had told me how, at the moment of his arrest, he had tried to save her from being incriminated by the document in his handwriting. The attractive Madame Volimacci, the hairdresser of La Madeleine, was never denounced by Cole. And when I talked to Madam Galant in Roubaix she said loyally, "Well, one thing for Paul, he never denounced me, either. After I was arrested, I realised from the questions that the Germans were asking me, that they had not been told anything at all about my real activities." How did Paul choose between those whom he decided to offer up as victims to the Germans and those whom he tried to save? Probably only a psychologist who was an expert in the ways of treason could answer that question. But it does seem that, at this stage at least, Paul Cole was trying to be chivalrous to Suzanne, by pretending that he wanted to have no more to do with her.

Having sent de Fliguë to the Gare du Nord with instructions to get rid of Suzanne, Cole went away with his two "British pilot" friends, promising to return later the same day. At half-past two that afternoon, Cole and the other two men turned up again at the apartment house at 6 Rue Quatrefages where de Fliguë lived with his wife, as did also, in another apartment, a further member of the network named Agnes Kirman, who had already aided Cole greatly by hiding British pilots on their way through Paris. That afternoon Cole found de Fliguë and Professor Holweck together and, without preliminaries he proposed to them, "Let's go over to the factory, where we can talk properly." The other two agreed, and Cole led the way down into the street.

All unsuspecting, de Fliguë and the Professor followed him. But the moment they stepped outside the house they realised that they had been betrayed. Waiting for them below was a party of German plain-clothes Security police, who covered the three men with revolvers. Paul made a half-hearted effort— was he just pretending, or was it a genuine escape attempt on his part?—to knock the gun from one of the policemen's hands, but he was quickly restrained. The Professor made a dash down the street and into a nearby garage, where he was cornered and captured. He and de Fliguë were bundled into a police car which had been waiting for them a little way down the street. As they drove off, de Fliguë saw Cole still standing on the pavement with the two men whom he had earlier introduced as British pilots but who, as de Fliguë now realised with horror, were in reality German police. "That was the instant," he told me many years afterwards, "when I realised that Cole had betrayed us."

The Germans took de Fliguë and the professor that afternoon first to a hotel in the Rue Caulaincourt, in Montmartre, which they used for interrogations, and gave them hours of questioning. Late that night they transferred them to the Santé prison. Next morning de Fliguë learned that Professor Holweck had tried to commit suicide. He knew too much, and possibly he was afraid that, under torture, he might be forced to talk.

The final fate of Professor Holweck is surrounded in mystery. All that is known definitely is that he died in prison within about two weeks of his arrest. During the war it was reported that he had died under torture during his interrogations. But it is more probable that he made a second suicide attempt which was successful, for when, some weeks later, de Fliguë himself was being interrogated, one of the questions he was asked by the Germans was, "Why did Professor Holweck kill himself?"—which was the first intimation he had that the professor was dead.

Monsieur de Fliguë himself was transferred from the Santé prison to the jail at Loos where the Germans had centred their inquiries into the Cole escape organisation. He stayed there for three months under interrogation and then was deported to Germany, first to Bochum, then to the concentration camp at Esterwegen, then to prison at Wolfenbuttel, where he stayed until April 1945, as one of the category of "Nacht und Nebel" prisoners scheduled for extermination. Finally he was liberated just in time by the Red Army who, when they discovered that he was of Russian origin, promptly arrested him again, though only temporarily. But his luck and his courage held, and at long last he returned once more to his home and factory in Paris, where he still carries on his business.

"And yet the odd thing was," said de Fliguë to me that day as he sat with me in the Paris restaurant looking back over the years, "that although Cole denounced me, I believe he never told the Germans more than a little of what I was really doing. I know he never told them, for instance, that I had sent to

Britain guidance for the bombing of the port of Lorient, which was later carried out by the R.A.F. My own view is that he betrayed as little as he could about me, in the hope that I would not talk too much about Suzanne."

*   *   *

It was the day after Paul Cole had thus assisted in the arrest of de Fliguë and Professor Holweck that he had turned up excitedly at the Chope du Pont Neuf and related to Suzanne and Durand his story of how the three of them had made their dramatic "escapes". But what his own position was at this moment is even to-day not clear. Had he, in fact, himself temporarily escaped from the clutches of his German masters, or was he, in coming to meet Suzanne and Durand at the restaurant, merely preparing another trap for two more chosen "victims"? And why did Paul, at the Chope du Pont Neuf, give Suzanne the obviously useless task of seeking clothes to help in the "escape" of the two men whom he knew in fact to be still in German hands? Presumably only to embellish his own story that he, and they, had evaded capture.

However this may be, it does seem certain that, when Cole and Suzanne fled together from the Chope du Pont Neuf the following evening—when Cole gave her the dramatic warning, "The Gestapo are after me"—his escape from his German captors was on that occasion a genuine one. At this moment he seems to have made one final determined effort to break the chain of treason, to disappear into hiding in some place where the Germans could not put him to further use, after his first series of betrayals.

Certain it is, anyway, that once Cole had gone into hiding with Suzanne in the flat of Tante Jeanne, the Abwehr had completely lost track of him. And they were tireless in their efforts to find him again. When they arrested M. Durand, the one question they asked him over and over again was "Where is Cole?"— a question which Durand was genuinely unable to answer.

And for many weeks, Vladimir de Fliguë, a prisoner in the harshly-lit offices in Lille of the Field Security Police, was pressed interminably with the same question, "Where is Cole? And where does that girl Suzanne live—for she might be able to lead us to him?" Once they offered de Fliguë his freedom if he would give them Suzanne's address (which he knew perfectly well). And once they threatened to shoot him if he did not. They hit him and they kept him short of food. But de Fliguë never mentioned a word about Tante Jeanne's flat—where that happy wedding party was taking place.

*　　*　　*

So Suzanne's personal tragedy was gradually unfolded.

In the days which followed her wedding she still had not the slightest hint that anything was seriously amiss with Paul Cole, not the least knowledge of his true background. Few people in the north even now, and none in Paris, had been warned about him. In the eyes of Suzanne, as in the eyes of many other people, Paul was still the gallant hero of the Resistance, on the run from the Germans, to be sure, but doing what he could to rebuild the broken network. She was sure she could trust him.

Meanwhile Cole's mysterious absences from Paris continued, and grew more frequent. Whenever Suzanne asked him about his trips, he always claimed to be rebuilding the network. What he was really doing at this time nobody knows. But it is indeed possible that Paul, having been arrested, having denounced at this time about twelve of his friends, and then having escaped again with Suzanne's aid, was making a genuine attempt to establish a new escape network with the aid of those of his contacts who had not been warned of his traitorous activities. He probably believed that those who were safely in the hands of the Gestapo would be unable to warn their friends about him and that in some way he could still save his reputation.

However that may be, Cole's apparent resumption of work,

Suzanne's excitement over her marriage to him, the attentions which he showed her and his gift for inspiring confidence made her dismiss from her mind the brief misgivings which had been aroused by the incidents of the missing brooch and the quarrel about the photograph.

But gradually, in the weeks succeeding their wedding, Suzanne began to feel a strange unease and restlessness. It was not that she for a moment suspected Cole of anything. But it seemed to her that she herself was being given no opportunity to push forward the work of the escape organisation which she had so much at heart.

"I'm rebuilding the network in my own way" was all he would ever say. "It's better that you don't know too much about it at this stage, Suzie. Just trust me."

And the more restless Suzanne became at her frustrating inactivity, the more Cole began to seek for new ways to keep her occupied. No doubt he feared that if he did not produce some convincing occupation for Suzanne she would again urge that they should travel together to Marseilles—a thing which Cole dared not do, for fear of running into those of his former associates such as Pat O'Leary or Roland Lepers who knew of his treachery.

Soon Cole hit on the ingenious plan of sending Suzanne on completely imaginary missions, assuring her that the work she was doing was vital to him in ways that only he, the British Intelligence expert, could understand. And her faith in him was still so great that she accepted all his assignments unquestioningly.

Thus one day Paul said to her, "Suzie, I want you to go to Brussels. I've got a message to deliver there and it's much too important to send by post."

Suzanne, welcoming any sort of resumption of activity, promptly agreed, though the journey through the German "Forbidden zone" of the north and into Belgium was certain to be a hard one. Cole produced a sheet of paper covered with groups of letters quite meaningless in themselves, but which he declared to be a form of secret code.

"Just memorise these, Suzy dear," he said. "Then, when you get to Brussels go somewhere where you can't be seen, write them all down again and mail them to the address which I will give you. And take great care that nothing goes wrong." Paul would explain no more.

Suzanne did exactly as she was told and, after a nightmare journey to Brussels, in which she passed a whole night on the platform of Lille station and nearly got herself arrested, she posted the letter to the address indicated by Paul. It was only later, when she showed the address to the British War Office to aid them in their inquiry into Cole's activities, that they told her that no such person and not even any such street in Brussels had ever existed. Cole had simply been trying to keep his ardent assistant busy, to get her out of the way in Paris. while he went about his own mysterious affairs.

On another occasion, Paul sent Suzanne down to the demarcation line at St. Martin-le-Beau, "just to see that everything is all right there," as he told her. It was; and Suzanne returned to Paris thinking that they could soon start normal work again and glad that she would soon once more be sharing fully in Paul's activities.

Then at last, one fine day in May, Paul announced that some real action was impending. He told her, "Suzanne, we've got another job to do. Three British pilots are coming to Paris from the north, and we are going together to take them down to Marseilles, along the usual route. I have found out that only Garrow has been arrested after all, so we can go to Marseilles quite safely."

But he explained that the plans for the journey were not going to be quite the same as usual. "I still have some very important business to do in Paris," Paul told Suzanne, "So you had better go on to Tours ahead of me, and meet every train from Paris until the British pilots show up. Then, if I'm not able to come along, if I'm still held up by my business in Paris, you can take them down to Marseilles yourself."

Suzanne agreed, but she never could have guessed what Paul's intended "business" really was. It was some four months later that she learnt the truth about Cole's final two days in Paris.

So off to Tours Suzanne went, and she waited there day after day for a week or more, meeting the trains, but seeing not the slightest sign of either Paul or the pilots. Finally she wrote a letter of protest to Paul, indignantly demanding to know what was happening. Instead of a reply from Paul himself, Suzanne received a letter from Tante Jeanne, obviously written at Paul's dictation—and it made Suzanne more angry than ever. For, in the slightly superior tone which Suzanne recognised as being unmistakably inspired by Cole, the letter admonished her not to be a silly and impatient little girl, to be grown up, adult, and learn to wait, and above all to trust the British officer who understood so much better than she did how matters should be run.

The sense of frustration felt by Suzanne was agonizing, and there was another reason for it besides the long days of lonely inactivity in Tours. Something had happened to Suzanne, and it was something which she needed urgently to talk to Paul about. But she forced herself to wait, meeting every train which came from Paris, and finally, about the end of May, a train steamed in to Tours and Paul stepped out of it, smiling as usual—but without any British pilots.

"Whatever has been happening?" asked Suzanne urgently, as the two walked together from the station.

And Paul airily explained: "Something went wrong in Paris —the pilots had to go south by another route. As for us, we've got to get out of occupied France—and quick. We will cross the demarcation line tonight, for Suzy, there isn't a moment to lose. I'll tell you all the details later on. This evening we must leave for St. Martin-le-Beau."

Suzanne asked no more questions at that moment. She was bursting to talk to Cole about her own personal affairs, to tell him the news which she had been hugging to herself through all the long and lonely wait in Tours, and which had been something too important and too personal to write. Now she suddenly burst out with it.

She said: "Paul, we are going to have a baby. I'm sure it's going to be a splendid son for you—he'll be just like you and I'll be so proud of him. I'd like to call him 'Patrick'."

Cole's face showed nothing of what he really felt at this news, and he made some conventional remark of congratulation. "We'll take care of everything once we get south, Suzy dear," was all he said.

But his mind was already feverishly working on a very different matter. For some reason, as Suzanne was soon to learn, Paul had turned against her. Even now he had a scheme which would seal the fate of herself and the unborn Patrick as well. What Cole's real motives can have been in adopting this plan, beyond his natural talent for treachery, can never be known. Perhaps Suzanne in her eagerness had been asking him too many questions, and Cole feared, quite wrongly, that she was already suspecting him, might soon become a danger to him. However that may be, the plan which he now adopted for "liquidating" her was diabolical.

The couple left Tours that evening for St. Martin-le-Beau, and supped together in the little home of M. Besnard. Calmly they discussed their immediate plans, and Suzanne suggested that they should call at Lyons on their way to Marseilles to see if her friend Jean Biche had any news of what had been happening in the South. Cole promptly agreed, and with the air of a man who has everything under perfect control, he added: "As a matter of fact I have an important job which you can do for me there."

From his pocket Cole produced a piece of thin paper with a

drawing on it—a plan of one of the main German fighter aero-dromes outside Paris. "If we can rush this to England soon," he told her, "the R.A.F. will be able to bomb the airport and destroy dozens of Nazi fighters. I want you to take it, Suzanne, and when we get to Lyons I'll give you an address where you must deliver it."

Suzanne took the piece of paper and guarded it carefully, delighted that Paul was again entrusting her with important work.

The crossing of the line went uneventfully, except that the couple were stopped on the far side by a French patrol. But this time both Paul and Suzanne had well-forged identity cards, provided by the Crépels in Paris, and a convincing cover-story to the effect that they were a French couple on their way to visit a sick relative in the south. After holding them for a while at their post, the French patrol finally let them go on their way.

Safely arrived in Lyons, Paul Cole took Suzanne to a double room on the top floor of the large Hotel Angleterre on the Place Carnot. They dined together in apparent harmony. Just before they went to bed that night Cole solicitously asked Suzanne, "The plan of the aerodrome—have you got it safely, Suzie dear?" Sleepily Suzanne replied that she had. This was the last night that she was to spend in Paul Cole's company.

*   *   *

Now, in Lyons, the pace of Suzanne Warren's personal drama suddenly quickens; the web of intrigue around her grows at once more complicated and more deadly. Two things happened simultaneously. Paul Cole proceeded stealthily with his private plan to rid himself of this newly-married wife and her unborn baby. But, all unknown to him, Cole himself was about to encounter a new and efficient personal enemy who was neither German nor British, but French. His name: Monsieur Louis Triffe.

At this moment of the war, Monsieur Triffe was the head for the Lyons area of the anti-espionage police service known as the "D.S.T." (for Direction de Surveillance du Territoire). Officially M. Triffe was working for the Vichy government, but secretly he was strongly pro-allied. And it happened that, through channels of his own, M. Triffe had heard of Paul Cole's activities and the constant menace which he represented to members of the French Resistance. M. Triffe resolved to arrest Cole as soon as he could lay hands on him and before he could do any further harm. And, as officials of the D.S.T. in France invariably do, M. Triffe acted with speed and efficiency.

It was very early in the morning after Paul and Suzanne had arrived at their Lyons hotel, and while they were both still asleep, that there came a powerful knocking at the door of their bedroom. When Paul unlocked it, two men forced their way inside, flashed passes and announced, "French police—you must come along with us."

"But why?"

"You are accused of being British agents—come, there is no time to lose."

"Well," said Suzanne, "you might at least wait outside while we get dressed." The two men agreed to do so.

Quickly Suzanne snatched up the incriminating thin paper with its aerodrome plan, chewed it and with some difficulty swallowed it. She helped Cole hide some other papers behind a mirror. Then they presented themselves to the two police-men and were taken to their headquarters.

Suzanne was not too perturbed that morning as she was led away. She felt that being caught in the Free Zone was in any case very much better than being arrested by the Gestapo. Moreover both Cole and she had excellent and convincing identity papers. Their cover story had been worked out by Paul in detail—that Cole was a Frenchman who had lived most of his life in America and had volunteered to come back to fight (this to explain his foreign accent) and that Suzanne had

H

recently married him in France. Suzanne believed that, if both of them stuck firmly to this story, there was a good chance of getting away with it.

She was not even greatly worried when, after arriving at the police station, she and Cole were taken away to different rooms to be interrogated separately. They would, in any case, she felt sure, be telling the Vichy police the same story.

And the interrogation on that first day was not particularly tough. The detectives asked Suzanne about her background, her family, her war-time activities—and about Cole. And they asked her repeatedly, "Are you or are you not a British agent?" Suzanne kept denying that she was—for she still had no idea, of course, of the real motive which the D.S.T. had in arresting them—that of putting an end to the treacherous activities of her husband.

That evening Suzanne was taken to the Depot St. Jean, the centre in Lyons where suspects were detained before they were committed to prison. She still felt reasonably self-composed, and wondered how soon it would be before she saw Paul again.

The next day the blow fell.

While, during her interrogation the following morning, she was continuing to deny glibly all accusations, one of the detectives suddenly leaned towards her and said with great sincerity and force, "Suzanne, why do you keep on trying to defend Paul Cole? *You must know perfectly well yourself that the man is a despicable traitor.*"

Suzanne could hardly believe she had heard correctly. In the face of her disbelief the detective repeated his allegation, and he went on; "Not only is Cole a traitor, but he was planning to denounce even you to the Germans."

"That can't possibly be true," said Suzanne. "Whatever do you mean?"

With complete incredulity she heard the detective's story—that the paper she had swallowed in her hotel bedroom two days earlier, the plan of the German fighter aerodrome, had been a genuine German document and part of Cole's plan to rid himself of Suzanne. For the men to whom he would have told her to deliver the paper in Lyons were, in fact, not resistance men but agents of the German Security police. They would have arrested Suzanne there and then and taken her off to occupied France for trial—and she would almost certainly have been shot. Cole had planned what he believed would be the perfect double-cross.

But as Suzanne listened to all of this, she came to a comforting conclusion. The whole thing was merely a far-fetched story which the detectives were making up in order to trick her into talking. How could they think she would be so stupid as to fall for such a hoary ruse? (She could not at that moment know, of course, that the D.S.T. were acting in the best interests of the allies by arresting Cole, and were also trying to find out whether Suzanne herself was his willing accomplice or, as was the case, his innocent victim.)

So back Suzanne went to her former denials. She was resolved to tell her questioners nothing. She would be loyal to Cole no matter what stories they made up about him. Yet the battle of wits between the detectives and Suzanne still went on for several days. And gradually one thing after another which the detectives told her began to make her grow uneasy. They seemed to know so much, so many things, too, that only Paul himself could have told them. They even knew the full address of Tante Jeanne. And they gave her all kinds of details, many of which she did not know herself, of the people whom Paul had denounced, how he had done it, where they had lived, exactly what services they had rendered to the escape organisation. Slowly Suzanne herself began to think over the things which had puzzled her about Paul. There had been the mystery of the missing brooch. There was the incident of the fake photograph which had led to their serious dispute. There had been Paul's strange refusal, which had irritated her at the time, to let her go and take the clothes herself to de Fliguë and the Professor after their alleged escape. "Trust me, Suzie, trust me" Paul had always said. Now at last she began to wonder whether she had indeed trusted him too much.

Then the detectives started a new line with her which suddenly made her resolve once more to keep silent, made her again suspect that they were trying to trick her. For they told her now, "Suzanne, you must give us the names and addresses of all the members of the organisation that you know—so that we can ourselves warn them against Paul Cole."

This, thought Suzanne, was going too far. How could she believe that the Vichy police would genuinely want to warn allied Resistance workers? Stubbornly she told her questioners, "I know nothing about all that—nothing at all."

"But if you won't help us," the detectives replied, "and people whom we could have warned get arrested by the Germans, the responsibility will be yours, not ours." Still Suzanne could not believe that they were sincere. When she was taken back to the Depot St. Jean that night she felt shaken, bewildered and exhausted. Her hair was unkempt, and she felt ill and weak from her pregnancy.

It was thus that, in the courtyard of the depot one evening, she was seen sitting and silently crying by a fellow-prisoner, a good-looking British officer named Bob Sheppard. The son of a French mother and a British father, from Horsham, Surrey, who lived in Nantes at the outbreak of the war, Sheppard had trained as a British agent and been parachuted near Lyons. But a double misfortune had resulted in his immediate capture. The first misfortune was that he happened to land straight on to the roof of the local gendarmerie. But the gendarmes below heard nothing and even then Bob Sheppard might have escaped detection except for the second stroke of ill-luck. This was that the lady who lived in the adjoining house happened that very night to be entertaining a man friend to whom she was not married. When she heard someone scraping about on the roof, she jumped to the conclusion that it was her husband returning

—and to protect herself she promptly telephoned the gendarmes next door telling them, "There's a burglar on the roof." So they investigated, and Bob Sheppard, along with five members of the French Resistance men who had formed his reception committee found themselves, like Suzanne, in the Depot St. Jean attached to the Lyons Palais de Justice.

The spectacle of the lonely girl crying in the courtyard aroused Bob Sheppard's immediate sympathy and he went over to Suzanne and asked what he could do to help. She jumped at the chance to talk to somebody English whom she felt immediately that she could trust, and she told him all her story, about Paul Cole and the allegations that the French were now making against him, and her own dilemma. Ought she to yield to the arguments of the French detectives and reveal the names of the people in the network or not? Could there be possibly any grain of truth in the frightful allegations they had made to her about her husband?

Bob Sheppard listened to Suzanne's story carefully, and gave her the reply which, in fact, she had expected.

"Don't be a bloody fool," said Bob. "They must be just trying to make you talk. Why, after the fall of France I escaped to Britain myself through the Ian Garrow network. Cole *can't* be a traitor."

Greatly comforted, Suzanne went to sleep that night determined to persist next day in her refusal to tell the police anything. She felt rather ashamed of herself for having suspected, even for a moment, that Paul could have been a traitor.

But when her interrogation was resumed again next morning, the police had a new shock in store for her.

"Suzanne," said the officer in charge, "whatever we tell you about Paul Cole you refuse to believe. But everything we have said is true. However, since you absolutely refuse to listen to us, perhaps you will believe what you hear from Cole himself. Now we are going to make *him* tell you."

They took Suzanne into an adjoining room and a few moments

later Paul Cole was led in handcuffed between two policemen. He looked a different man from the debonair figure she had last seen in the hotel bedroom. He was haggard, and he avoided meeting Suzanne's eyes.

One of the detectives, without a preliminary word, went over to Cole and slapped his face, hard, twice.

"Now, you swine," he said, "tell this woman that you are just a dirty traitor. Go down on your knees and ask her to forgive you for what you have done to her."

Suzanne went white and felt her heart almost stop beating as she saw Cole, his suave mask dropped and all pretence of self-control abandoned, drop down on his knees and plead with her—in an unbelievable and abject scene.

The man whom until then she had known only as a gallant and fearless British officer, the man she had so happily married, now started to weep. He raised his hands and he cried in a piteous, thin, pleading voice, "Suzanne, it's true, I am a traitor. Everything they say is true. I don't know why—I don't know why I did it. But you know I love you, really. I'll do anything, anything, if you'll only forgive me."

One of the detectives checked him. "Speak French," he ordered, and Cole continued to babble on in broken French, with tears streaming down his face.

Suzanne put her hands to her face and turned away from him. There seemed nothing she could say.

Everything she had valued had suddenly collapsed into emptiness; patriotism, courage, trust and love—they all seemed just meaningless words now.

The detectives took Cole away. They had almost to drag him to his feet to make him walk from the room, still pleading and explaining incoherently.

Back at the Depot St. Jean that evening Suzanne did not speak to anybody, not even to Bob Sheppard. She sat alone in her cell clasping and unclasping her hands. She went over and over in her mind all that she and Paul had done together, all the things he had said. Many things were suddenly and cruelly clear to her now—the reason why Paul had never allowed her to see Ian Garrow in Marseilles, so that he could take all the credit for having brought British soldiers to safety, the reason why he had tried to keep her busy while he went about his own mysterious affairs, the reason why, after his arrest by the Germans and his betrayals, he had avoided going back to Marseilles and meeting those colleagues in the network who knew him as a traitor. And the abject scene that afternoon of Paul's "confession"—she had never thought to see a man behave in such a way.

Suzanne wept in her cell all through that night.

* * *

The head of the D.S.T. in Lyons, M. Louis Triffe, who had ordered the arrest of Cole and Suzanne, was a patriotic and honest Frenchman—but the case of Suzanne Warren presented him with a serious dilemma.

On the one hand he had no wish to bring an innocent girl before a court-martial, even a Vichy-French one. On the other hand his actions were open to close inspection by the Vichy authorities, many of whom were strongly Pétainist in their views, so that he obviously could not openly flout official procedures. Moreover, before he made any move, he wanted to be certain that Suzanne really was as innocent as she appeared to be, that she genuinely had known nothing of Paul's treacherous activities.

He even confided his doubts to Bob Sheppard, whom he knew often chatted with Suzanne in the evenings at the Depot St. Jean.

Bob Sheppard assured Triffe that he was certain that Suzanne was absolutely genuine, and gradually, after continuing her interrogations, the French officer reached the same conviction. But he could not legally set her free without the authority of a French magistrate.

So, after some days more in the Depot St. Jean, Suzanne was taken before an examining magistrate in the Lyons Palais de Justice, and Monsieur Triffe supported the plea that there was no real case against Suzanne and that she should therefore be discharged. But his plea was not successful. After listening carefully to the evidence, the examining magistrate exclaimed impatiently, "But this girl has admitted that she worked for the British; certainly she should be put on trial. Take her away." Reluctantly M. Triffe concurred.

But for Suzanne there was first a new ordeal to be faced before her trial. Because she had now been committed for trial, she was transferred from the comparatively easy-going atmosphere of the Depot St. Jean to the rigours of full imprisonment in the grim Lyons prison of St. Joseph. And now, in her deep personal distress, she had no longer even anybody to whom she could talk, for she was thrown into solitary confinement.

Suzanne's world now became a little cell with a door of plain wood in which there was a tiny hole to enable the wardresses to inspect her at any time of day or night. The cell itself was sparsely furnished, just a camp bed with a couple of blankets, a bucket for her personal needs, and a pitcher of water. The only human being she ever saw was the stern-faced wardress who, three times a day, opened her door to push inside her meals, and the wardress, apparently on instructions, never spoke to her. The food was wretched; coffee of grilled barley, which looked like dirty water, and soup with a few bits of swede floating in it and a chunk of black bread. Later when the prison authorities discovered that Suzanne was pregnant, they allowed her to have, once a week, a small piece of meat floating in her evening soup.

Worst of all was the little peep-hole in the door through which people came and inspected her. She never knew when she was or was not being watched. It became an obsession with her, and she would keep looking at the little hole, wondering whether any human eye was on the other side of it, and if so whose it was. It nearly drove her crazy.

And then there was Paul. The thought of him was with her day and night, and she could think of nothing else. Her mind was filled with doubts and questionings. Was he truly a traitor? Or had she been tricked by the police into misjudging him terribly? Surely the things they had said about him— that he had said about himself in that moment of abject confession—could not possibly be true? And in any case what was now going to become of her baby—the child of Paul Cole?

Questions like these went round and round in Suzanne's head. She tried to drive them away by clinging to happier thoughts of her past, the sunny sands of Frinton, the good comradeship of Tommy Edgar and the other British soldiers she had helped to escape and how recklessly they had sung English songs in the train as they journeyed south. One evening the wardress, looking through the peep-hole saw Suzanne sitting up in her bunk and singing, "Pack up Your Troubles in your Old Kit Bag—and smile, smile, smile!" To the wardresses she appeared to have gone mad. In fact that was only Suzanne's way of keeping sane—by building up a little world of her own around herself in her small dark cell.

After six weeks they took her out of solitary confinement and put her into a cell with two other women. One of them had been the mistress of a British agent; the other was under arrest for having given some secret French papers to the Germans. Such was the confusion of Vichy justice at that time. But when the woman who had aided the Germans heard that Suzanne was under arrest for having helped a British officer, she told her, "You're lucky. If it's the British you've been helping you'll be free in no time!" And after her six weeks of solitary confinement, Suzanne was glad of a chance to speak even to a German collaborator.

Some days later a dark blue prison van took Suzanne from the prison to the Fort Monluc for her court-martial, and here she saw Paul Cole once more.

It was a strange meeting. Suzanne was sitting in an ante-room to the court where the French officers were to sit in judgment on her, when suddenly Paul was brought in by two ordinary policemen. And, to Suzanne's astonishment, he seemed completely to have recovered his composure, to have changed his personality once more and have become again the self-possessed "British officer" whom she had known when she had married him. He wore a tidy grey suit, was neatly shaved and showed no particular sign of strain.

Suzanne rose to her feet and went towards Cole. The police-men paid no particular attention as she said to him softly in English, "Paul, tell me quickly, why did you do it?"

With, apparently, all his old self-assurance, Paul Cole whispered his urgent reply. "Of course I didn't do it, Suzie. How could you believe such things of a man like me? But I had to pretend to make a 'confession' in front of the Deuxième Bureau, for reasons which I can't explain to you just now. I'm astonished that you of all people should have thought there was a word of truth in what I said. Good acting, wasn't it? But all I ask now is that if you still have any doubts about me, wait until you get out of prison, then go to Geneva and contact the British Consulate there. There's a Colonel who works there who can tell you that I truly am a British agent. And you can tell him everything that has happened to me."

They were able to talk for only two minutes. Then policemen came and led Cole towards the court-room. As he went Suzanne began once more to feel slightly reassured. A small hope grew inside her; perhaps her husband was not a traitor after all.

But that hope was soon dashed when Suzanne followed Cole into the big court-room and was allowed to stand at the back and listen to his trial.

It was a room with high windows and at one end was a long table, at which sat a row of French officers in uniform. In front of the table was a stand at which Paul was placed. The officer who acted as prosecutor was on Paul's left.

And then Suzanne, standing with a crowd of people tightly-packed together at the rear of the court, listened with dismay as the story of Cole's treachery was unfolded in detail and with military precision. The romantic figure of Cole was efficiently and ruthlessly stripped bare.

Paul himself denied everything, of course. At the beginning of the proceedings he told the court in a firm, convincing voice, "I am a British Officer who always fought for my country. I have never betrayed a soul." But gradually he faltered under relentless questioning by the prosecuting officer, and on hearing the testimony given against him by the head of the D.S.T. The case against him was overwhelming. And Suzanne heard the officer-President of the court-martial formally condemn Cole to death "for delivering Frenchmen into the hands of the Germans." For once, Cole maintained his dignity, and he showed no special emotion as he turned smartly and walked from the court. He did not even glance at the woman who had become his wife, and whom, too, he had tried to deliver to the Germans.

Then Suzanne heard a court official call out her own name; "Suzanne Warenghem", and she was led forward to take the place of Cole on the stand.

Her own trial did not take long. The President asked her, "Is it true that you worked to aid a British escape network?" and Suzanne frankly admitted it, for there seemed no point in doing anything else. But she told the court, "My Father fought in the first World War, and when the second one came, and I saw my country occupied, it seemed to me to be my duty to help in any way I could—and that's why I did what I did."

"Did you ever suspect that Cole was a traitor," Suzanne was asked. "Never," she replied.

Monsieur Triffe himself gave evidence on Suzanne's behalf. He said that, after long enquiry by the D.S.T., he had become convinced that Suzanne had been the completely innocent victim of Paul Cole, that she had certainly never known the truth about him and that she had already suffered terribly through that man. In his view, she should be released immediately.

Even the prosecuting officer appeared to be moved by the sight of the attractive but haggard young woman, about to become a mother, who was before him. For he told the judges that he, too, took the view that Suzanne was a young girl who had already suffered enough. He would press no charges against her, he said, and he concluded with the plea, which struck Suzanne as odd though well-intentioned; "This young girl should not be punished for her mis-placed patriotism in helping allied soldiers to escape."

Without further discussion Suzanne was acquitted. She was taken to an empty prison cell for the formalities of release, and that same evening the prison gates were opened for her. She was free—but sick, anxious and completely alone.

Paul Cole remained for weeks inside the Fort Monluc, awaiting confirmation of his death sentence. And now he had lost every trace of his debonair self-assurance. His head was shaven and he was made to change his neat grey suit for a rough and ill-fitting khaki uniform.

One of the people who saw Cole in prison at this time was Bob Sheppard, who met him at the showers in Fort Monluc. On finding that Sheppard was British, Cole immediately tried to make friends with him, telling him his usual story.

"I'm a British officer, too, old boy. Got caught running a big escape network. What's the news from the outside world? Here, have an apple."

Paul offered Sheppard an apple which he had scrounged from somewhere inside the prison. But Sheppard would have nothing to do with him.

But for Suzanne, as Sheppard later told me, he had formed a high opinion from the moment he had first seen her crying in the prison courtyard. "She had guts, that girl," he recalled with admiration. "I used to wonder, afterwards, how she managed to keep herself going during all those bad times. I think it was basically her pride—pride in the best sense of the word. Her head was bloody but unbowed and she just would not give in. Like so many people of northern France, she was really upset by the war, and determined to do something about it. And of course, she was very young."

*   *   *

Suzanne stumbled out through the gates of the prison that evening in late August, 1942, almost in a trance. She had no idea what to do. She had nowhere to go, no husband with her now, very little money and, above all the agonising certainty that her baby was due to be born within about the next three months. People turned and stared, that fine summer night, at the spectacle of the dishevelled girl, weeping silently to herself, as she wandered through the streets of Lyons.

Finally Suzanne remembered Jean Biche, from whom—how long ago it seemed—she had once taken Colonel Seagrim on the escape-route to Marseilles, one of the first jobs she had done for the Ian Garrow organisation. Jean Biche lived at the big Royal Hotel, on the Place Bellecour, and it was there that Suzanne decided to go. But when she got there, she found that Jean Biche was out for the evening so there was nothing for her to do but sit and wait for his return. She settled down in one corner of the lounge—the first time she had sat in a soft chair for many weeks—and suddenly she began weeping again.

It was thus that Jean Biche found her, and he was full of sympathy when he heard her story. The hotel was packed with guests and there was no bedroom free. So Jean Biche arranged for a bed to be put up in a sitting-room for her, gave her food, and sat until late in the night trying, vainly, to offer her some comfort. But when he had gone, Suzanne spent nearly all the rest of that night weeping by herself in the darkness.

Obviously Suzanne was badly in need of aid, rest and friendship. So after a few days it was arranged that she should go to stay in the country with a former Paris schoolteacher named Mademoiselle Demeure, who had been a member of the network, had been herself denounced by Paul, but had escaped. It was a relief for Suzanne to be able to talk to somebody who had also known Paul, and for a fortnight the two women stayed in a little village outside Lyons while Suzanne regained her strength. But Suzanne was in too great a state of nervous tension to remain inactive long. "I must get down to Marseilles," she told her friend. "The organisation there will help me get out of France. And I want my baby safe in England."

Already she was making plans for the baby she was sure would be a son. She would never tell him anything about his father except that he was an Englishman who had died during the war. She would give him every chance that lay in her power to have a decent life.

Down in Marseilles, Suzanne discovered that among the members of the escape organisation who were still free and working there were Dr. Rodocanachi and the elegant and kindly Greek, Mario Prassinos. They did everything they could for her. They found her a tiny bedroom in a cheap hotel where she could stay, they gave her a small allowance from the organisation's scanty funds; Mario sent her flowers and sometimes in the evenings would call and take her out to dine on Marseilles bouillabaisse in a better restaurant than she herself could have afforded.

Suzanne's most urgent concern now was that everybody in the network should be warned of Paul Cole's treachery. Both Mario and Dr. Rodocanachi, she found, knew about it already. She gave them a list of all the other people she knew, so that they, too, could be alerted about Cole's activities. She had already written from Lyons to Tante Jeanne in Paris, so that she could pass on a warning about Cole to other members of the network she knew. And now in Marseilles she received an answer from Tante Jeanne which gave her, about four months late, a piece of new and even more shattering information about

Paul Cole. It revealed the secret of what Cole had really been doing in those last days in Paris while she had been waiting for him so impatiently in Tours. It was a story not of Resistance, but of robbery—and the people whom Cole had chosen for his victims were those very ones who, in his hours of need, had cared for him like a member of their own family—Suzanne's three elderly aunts.

Tante Jeanne's letter, carefully worded, gave Suzanne only the bare facts of what had happened, but they were enough to arouse her to fresh indignation and despair at Paul's treachery. Years later, after the war, I myself was told the details of this exploit by Tante Marie and Tante Isabelle themselves, when I went to visit them in Paris.

Paul's plot had begun, it seemed, only a few days after Tante Jeanne had, so obediently at his request, written to Suzanne in Tours admonishing her to wait on there and trust in Cole completely. One morning Paul had come to the elderly French-woman and had told her, "Tante Jeanne, I need some help from you, since Suzanne is away."

He related to her that three British pilots had arrived from the north and were hidden in the Hotel St. Nicholas, far away on the other side of Paris, near the Bastille. The men, he said, were seriously wounded and badly in need of help. "Could you go and dress their wounds," Paul urged, "and patch them up a bit so that they can be fit to make the journey south to Marseilles?"

Without hesitation the good-hearted Frenchwoman agreed. She put together dressings, bandages and iodine in her bag, and hurried off from Becon-les-Bruyères on the long journey across Paris to the Bastille. When she reached the hotel, there was no sign of any British pilots. Supposing that they had not yet arrived, Tante Jeanne settled down to wait until they came.

The previous evening, Cole had made a somewhat similar plea to Tante Marie. He told her, "Tante Marie, I have three wounded British pilots coming down from the north tomorrow and they have nowhere to go. Could you be really wonderful and let me put them in your flat —just for the morning, until I can get them away? You had better not be there yourself—it will be safer that way. Just give me the key of your front door and be out of the house by nine o'clock, and I will look after everything."

Tante Marie not only agreed but got up early that day to have plenty of time to spread her table with things for the British pilots to eat and drink and to write a welcoming notice in soap across the big mirror in her salon; "Welcome to the Brave." Then she left her flat, slammed the door behind her and went off to the office of the big pharmaceutical firm where she has worked all her life.

Tante Isabelle, too, had received a call from Cole, but to her he had recounted a different story, this time about the Abbé Carpentier—who had been in prison for nearly six months.

"Can you help us out, Tante Isa," Paul had asked her. "My friend the Abbé Carpentier has escaped and is coming to Paris this afternoon, and he needs somewhere safe to sleep. Could you go over and see your friend the Abbé Amy and ask him if he can put up the Abbé Carpentier and also give him 20,000 francs (just over £100) on my behalf. I'm sorry to trouble you, but it's urgent and the British Intelligence Service will be most grateful if you can do it."

Tante Isabelle, who had just come in from doing her marketing, said, "Well, Paul, I don't know whether the Abbé Amy will be at home, but I'll go and try to see him if it's really important."

"It's terrifically important," said Paul earnestly. "And by the way, if you have two keys to your flat, you might leave me one of them, so that I can come back this evening and wait for you here."

So, trustingly, Tante Isabelle handed Cole one of her latch-keys and prepared to set off on the long journey across Paris to the suburb of Malakoff, to contact the Abbé Amy. As Paul stood by watching her taking her best necklace from her jewel-box, and putting on two of her best rings, he chided her banter-ingly, "Oh, Tante Isabelle, you don't need to put on all that jewellery just to see the Abbé Amy." It was only later that she understood the significance of that remark.

At Malakoff, Tante Isabelle found the good Abbé in his vestry, and together they waited all through the afternoon for the expected arrival of the Abbé Carpentier, who in fact at just about this time was being transferred from the prison at Loos on the terrible trip to Germany from which he never returned.

With all the three old ladies thus safely out of the way on the false missions with which he had entrusted them, Paul was able to devote his day to a leisurely and painstaking rifling of all their three apartments. From Tante Jeanne he took her family heirlooms of jewellery and silverware—and he had lived long enough in her flat to know exactly where everything was kept. From Tante Isabelle he took a wallet full of money from her desk and all the jewellery except that which she had fortu-nately put on before she went to see the Abbé Amy. From Tante Marie he took jewels, watches and old silver—and even, as a final touch of meanness, the few tins of condensed milk which the old lady had managed to collect in those days of extreme food shortages.

Tante Marie, returning from her work at the office, was the first of the three to reach her flat, which she believed to have been occupied during her absence by the escaping British pilots. She did not discover Paul's theft at once, because, before he had decamped, he had left a cunning little note for her behind him on the sitting-room table.

"Dear Tante Marie," said the note, "One of the boys has been very naughty and I was not able to make him give up the key of your wardrobe, which is still locked. But if you will come over to the St. Nicholas hotel where I am staying this evening, I will give it to you."

So, slightly exasperated, Tante Marie went into Paris again

I

and called at the hotel which Paul had mentioned. When she got there she was told, "Sorry, there's no such gentleman here just now." But her needless trip had given Paul just that much extra time before Tante Marie discovered that she had been robbed, and before she could warn the other two aunts.

Next, returning late that evening from the suburb of Malakoff, came Tante Isabelle. She went to a desk and could not find her wallet. Then she went over to Tante Jeanne's apartment and was surprised to find that, although it was nine o'clock at night, her sister had not come home. Finally she went back to her own flat, and discovered the full extent of the robbery.

But strangest of all was the experience of Tante Jeanne, who had waited in vain all day at the hotel near the Bastille for the arrival of the British pilots. For late that same evening, just as she was thinking of giving up and returning to her home, Paul Cole himself walked in.

He earnestly explained, "I'm sorry, Tante Jeanne, to have made you waste all this day, but something went wrong with the British pilots and they had to travel by another route. But never mind, let me make it up to you by offering you a good dinner."

In his hand Paul was carrying a bulky brief-case and he kept this carefully by his side throughout the dinner, which they had in a restaurant in the centre of Paris. Afterwards the three aunts agreed that the brief-case must have contained the very articles which Paul had stolen from them, and which he was planning to pawn before he went off to Tours to meet Suzanne. The dinner which Paul, thus newly-enriched, offered to Tante Jeanne was the best that could be got at that moment in war-time Paris. He offered her a bottle of good wine and then, perhaps under its mellowing influence, he did a very strange thing. With tears welling up in his eyes, Paul Cole leaned forward across the table and clasped the elderly Frenchwoman by the hand. "Tante Jeanne," he said softly, looking her straight in the eyes, "please forgive me for all I have done—I would like to feel that I have your pardon."

The practical Tante Jeanne thought Paul must be play-acting. "Don't be silly, my dear Paul," she said, "whatever are you talking about?"

It was only after she got back to her flat late that night that she discovered. And she never saw Paul Cole again.

*   *   *

All this, in bare outline, Suzanne now learned about in Marseilles through the letter from Tante Jeanne. She promptly sat down and wrote to Paul Cole in prison a letter which made no attempt to be carefully worded, but which, if he had had any sense of shame, should surely have shamed him. "It seems that it isn't enough," wrote Suzanne bitterly, "to be a traitor, and to have made love to every woman in the network—you even had to rob three old ladies who had risked their very necks to shelter you." But this letter remained unanswered.

The cold winter weeks which followed for Suzanne in Marseilles were, despite the efforts of her friends, times of agonizing loneliness, disillusionment and frustration. Everything on which she had pinned her hopes and her faith seemed to have collapsed around her. She had no real work to do and at that moment she had no wish to resume her Resistance activities, after having just burned her fingers so badly. She was so disillusioned that she felt there was nobody whom she could completely trust. Her one ambition was to get to Britain before her baby was born. The baby was now all she had to live for.

Here, too, there was nothing but frustration. The members of the organisation told her frankly that, in view of her condition, they dared not let her take the risk of attempting the dangerous and arduous journey across the Pyrenees. If she fell ill and collapsed in the mountains she would be a peril not only to herself, but to all the other members of the escaping group as well. They did not seem anxious, either, to let her travel by the alternative route which was being used for escapes at that time, a felucca which left Marseilles at dead of night and made its way to Gibraltar. Several left while Suzanne was waiting in Marseilles, one carrying nearly a hundred people, but Suzanne was never taken along. There was nothing for her to do except sit in cheap restaurants eating the miserable war-time meals which they provided—at that time usually little more than grey noodles and a vegetable—or else to sit alone in her tiny hotel bedroom. And wait, and wait.

The baby was not due to be born before mid-December and from one day to another Suzanne postponed making any visit to a doctor. Then, suddenly, in the last week of October, she realised that she ought to go. Dr. Rodocanachi put her in touch with one of the best clinics in Marseilles and promised that the organisation would pay her bill. On the very next day her pains began, and Suzanne was rushed to the clinic. She had a bad time there, partly due to her own weakened condition and partly to the fact that it was not the practice in France at that time to give a mother anaesthetic, which was held to be harmful to the child. But finally, on October 30, 1942, her son Patrick was born.

He had light brown hair and blue eyes and, despite all his mother had been through, he seemed a healthy and happy baby. Suzanne spent a week with him in the clinic, just one week of satisfaction and hope, before she had to leave.

And now her troubles began again. The dingy hotel in which she had her tiny room did not accept babies. They did not want Patrick. They feared that he would disturb the other guests in the house which, like most second-rate French hotels, was built with paper-thin walls. Suzanne had been given the address of a mid-wife, and regretfully she decided to let Patrick be boarded out with her, while she tried to find some other accommodation in the over-crowded city. The mid-wife seemed a suitable woman, for she had two well-fed children of her own. Every day Suzanne visited the mid-wife's house, wrapped Patrick in a shawl, and took him out for a walk, carrying him in her arms through the busy Marseilles streets, because she could not afford a pram. One day a street photographer took a picture of her as she walked with the baby, herself bare-legged except for white woollen socks, and with a scarf around her thick brown hair. She bought the picture from the man—and to-day it is the only sad souvenir which she still has of Patrick.

She wrote another letter to Paul Cole in Fort Monluc, telling him of the birth of his son. But he never answered—or else was not allowed to answer.

Soon, Suzanne began to grow anxious about the health of her baby. He seemed listless, unhappy, and, physically, he made no progress at all. Each week, she took him to a hospital to be put on the scales, only to find to her dismay that he was gaining no weight whatsoever. She could not understand it, for on her ration-card she was entitled as a mother to a special allowance of tinned milk for her baby, and this she regularly bought and handed over to the mid-wife who was looking after him.

Finally she discovered the reason for Patrick's weakness—and it was one which, almost as much as the affair of Cole, shook her faith in human nature. One day at the mid-wife's house Suzanne commented to the maidservant there on the baby's poor condition. The girl gave her an odd look. "Maybe he'd do better if he was getting his proper food," she said.

"Whatever do you mean?" asked Suzanne.

"It's not for me to say anything," replied the girl, mysteriously. "But if I was that baby's mother I'd try and find out what was happening to his milk."

Suzanne made inquiries and to her horror she found out the secret. The mid-wife to whom she had entrusted Patrick—although she herself was the mother of two children—had been selling the baby's tins of condensed milk on the black market. Suzanne stormed in to the woman and in a fit almost of desperation took Patrick straight out of the house.

With Patrick in her arms she went back to her little hotel and pleaded with the manageress to allow her to keep her baby with her, at least for a few nights until she could find a room somewhere else. "Very well," said the woman. "I don't mind stretching a point just for once. But if your baby cries at night and disturbs the other guests, I'm afraid you'll both have to leave."

Suzanne carried Patrick up to her room, improvised a little cot for him, and after that she nursed him herself night and day.

But the conditions in which they were living were desperately hard. It was a bitterly cold winter and because of war-time shortages there was no heating whatever in the hotel. Suzanne's little room was soon festooned with cold damp nappies which refused to dry. She had to leave Patrick alone whenever she hurried out to do a little shopping. Once when he seemed to have caught a chill, she was not able even to buy a thermometer to check his temperature, because there were none in the war-time shops. And always, every time the baby cried, Suzanne was terrified that some guest would complain and that they would be turned out of the hotel.

Christmas Day came, Patrick's first Christmas, a grim cold day which brought Suzanne little comfort. But she did her best: she bought a tiny crib, a small sprig of a Christmas tree and one little toy for Patrick, and when he saw the little figures of the crib, the baby did indeed seem to smile.

But all Suzanne's efforts failed to produce another room in which the two could live—and she was not able to search very much because she could not leave Patrick long alone. Again she pleaded with her friends in the escape organisation to be sent with the baby to England. They could go by boat to Gibraltar, she argued, and perhaps Patrick could be given something to make him sleep during the time they were smuggling him on board the felucca. Her friends promised to see what they could do. But their help seemed a long time coming.

In the last week of January Patrick fell ill again. He was restless and in obvious discomfort, but he did not seem to have a fever as Suzanne settled him to sleep on the night of January 23 in the little unheated hotel room. She wrapped him up as warmly as she could and gave him his last bottle for the night, but Patrick did not seem to be very hungry. Then Suzanne herself crept into bed shivering, and turned out the light.

During that night she heard Patrick whimpering softly once or twice, but he never made any serious noise and in the early morning he fell completely silent, asleep as Suzanne thankfully believed. It was only when she got up and went over to give him his bottle later that morning that she discovered that Patrick was dead.

*   *   *

It probably was that pride of which Bob Sheppard had spoken that kept Suzanne Warren alive in the days immediately following the death of her baby. Many another girl suffering in quick succession two such blows as the treason of her husband and the death of her child, and herself weakened by imprisonment and under-nourishment, might well at that stage have contemplated self-destruction. But some innate courage in Suzanne's character gave her the strength to keep going, and made her refuse to bow her head before the bludgeonings of fate. Despite all she had experienced, she was, even now, only just over twenty-one years old. With the courage of youth, she determined that she would not give in—never, whatever happened. So, stoically, she watched one cold January morning, as Patrick was put into his little grave, and had the spot marked with a wooden cross because at that moment Suzanne had not enough money even to provide him with a grave-stone.

By now the Germans occupied all France, having used the excuse of the Allied landings in North Africa in November 1942 to take over the whole country. Even earlier, however, they had infiltrated into the nominally "unoccupied zone".

Suzanne resolved to get out of Marseilles as quickly as she could, for it had become for her a city of hateful memories. In Lyons she had two loyal friends, Roger Berthier and his wife Fernande, both of them active Resistance workers. Roger, a genial little man, specialised in receiving explosives parachuted by the R.A.F. and storing them underneath his bed until such time as he could put them to good use in blowing up railway trains. Suzanne had met him in the prison at Lyons, when he had been arrested as one of the members of Bob Sheppard's reception committee. Fernande was a member of an information network. So Suzanne proposed, and Fernande gladly agreed, that she should move in and stay for a while with her in her small apartment in the Villeurbane suburb of Lyons. Simultaneously, because she was needing every personal contact and every friend she could find, she wrote to Bob Sheppard, telling him all that had happened. Because of a mild attack of diptheria, Sheppard had been transferred from the Fort Monluc prison to the Hopital de la Croix Rousse, where the nurses and doctors conspired, with false thermometer readings, to disguise his case as a serious one while he secretly prepared to escape. Suzanne had corresponded fairly regularly with Sheppard at this time, and had sent him a few food parcels in hospital. Sheppard, lonely too, kept her letters and her photograph by his bedside—and all unwittingly contributed thereby to Suzanne's new ordeal.

Now it was the beginning of February, and thanks to the friendly sympathy of Fernande Berthier, Suzanne was just beginning to feel a little more self-composed. But one morning, glancing out of the window of Fernande's apartment, she saw two men approaching the house whom she recognised at once as being plain-clothes policemen. In the flat were some letters from Robert Sheppard and a list of all the B.B.C. news broadcasts and also a set of false identity cards. Suzanne quickly threw all these papers into the stove before she opened the door to the two men.

"We are arresting you," said one of the policemen.

"Whatever for?"

"For helping a British officer to escape."

"What on earth do you mean? What British officer?"

"Captain Robert Sheppard, who escaped from the Hopital de la Croix Rousse two nights ago."

Suzanne almost laughed in their faces. For months, back in 1941, she had helped British soldiers to escape, and had never been caught. Now, it seemed, she was to be arrested for something she had not done, and at the one period of her war-time career when she had definitely not been engaging in Resistance activities of any kind.

"This is too ridiculous," she told the policemen, who, however, insisted that she should accompany them to their headquarters.

Even now Suzanne did not feel greatly alarmed. She supposed some mistake had been made which would rapidly be cleared up and that she would be back in Fernande's apartment by the same evening. As they walked to the police station she began to talk to the detectives, who, she found, were not personally unfriendly to her. "You ought to be ashamed of yourselves," she told the two young men, "two good Frenchmen doing the work of the Germans. Why don't you let me escape?"

"We don't like this job any more than you would," replied one of the detectives. "But if we let you escape, we would be the ones who would suffer." And after a little further talk along the same lines, he suddenly said, "But if you would like to promise to help us get to England through your escape organisation, we might come with you and then we could all escape together."

But Suzanne feared a trick. Perhaps they were only trying to find out about the Marseilles organisation and what her contacts with it were. So she said to the men, "No, just let me escape. I can't help you because I don't belong to any organisation." But the men would not agree, and so they finally took her to the police station. She was allowed to telephone to

Fernande, who came at once, and the two girls spent most of the night together, sitting side-by-side on the hard wooden bench of the police station and talking in low tones. It was uncomfortable but convenient, because it enabled them to cook up together the stories they would tell when they were interrogated.

Suzanne's first morning of interrogation went easily enough. It was done by French officials of the Vichy police as a matter of routine. They politely asked her questions about herself, and whether she had actually helped Bob Sheppard to escape, as he had done, from the hospital ward. She told them the whole thing was an unfortunate coincidence, that she had in fact written to Sheppard quite openly from Marseilles and Lyons, had even sent him a food parcel or two, but had absolutely nothing to do with his escape. And without commenting, the Vichy police took note of what she said.

But that same afternoon, Suzanne was handed over to another set of police, Pétainists and Germans working openly together, now that there was no longer an "unoccupied zone", and from that moment on her situation grew really serious.

She was led into an office in which were two Germans in civilian clothes and one German Security guard in uniform. At first the Germans were soft and civil in their interrogation of Suzanne. They tried the method of sweet persuasion. They realised, they told her, that she was only a young girl who could not understand the full significance of what she had been doing. They had no wish to be hard on her. If she would tell them the names of all the people she knew in the escape organisation, they would say no more to her and let her go.

"In any case," said one of the Germans, "we already know most of the names, so you will not even be doing anybody any harm by talking to us."

This, as Suzanne guessed, was a flat lie. In fact, when the Germans moved into unoccupied France in the previous

November, the pro-allied officials of the French police had patriotically destroyed all the records they had about the Resistance, so as to prevent them falling into German hands. So their dossiers at least contained nothing, for instance, of what Cole and Suzanne had told to Monsieur Triffe.

At that moment Suzanne was probably the big hope of the Germans in their efforts to track down all the men still at liberty who were behind the Marseilles escape route. But she told them nothing. "I don't know a thing," she assured them.

"You are wrong, and very unwise, Mademoiselle," said the German in charge. "Listen, if you give us the names of all the people that you yourself worked with, we can arrest them quietly and calmly and thus avoid bloodshed. Nobody will ever need to know that it was you who gave us the names—and if you help us, we will help you." It was probably exactly the same argument as they had once used so successfully with Paul Cole.

For several days after that, Suzanne was taken to the same office, and the same bait was laid for her in the same tender trap. Once the German officer pointed to the shabby clothes which Suzanne was wearing. "A pretty girl like you," said he, "it's a shame that you should have to go around in such an outfit. Wouldn't you like to have some clothes? We could easily help you there, you know."

"Besides," went on the German, "you would actually be helping your country if you collaborate with us. You ought to realise that the whole of France is occupied now, and the French people who work with us are only helping to promote peace and understanding between our two great nations. France's future is now indissolubly united with that of the German Reich. Why don't people like you understand these things?"

"I'm sorry," said Suzanne, "but I just don't believe that is true."

Then they tried a new line. They asked her suddenly, "By

the way, where have you been getting the money from on which you have been living in Marseilles all this time?"

Suzanne tried to think quickly, though she was feeling very tired. She told the Germans, "My Father sent me some money—he sent it down from Le Havre to Marseilles by a friend." (She could not say she had received it by postal order, for fear the Germans would have checked with the Marseilles post office and found no postal order there.)

In fact, the Germans did check in Le Havre with Suzanne's father, and here the quick wits and good nature of a French police official did much to help her. From Lyons the Germans sent a report on Suzanne's claim to have received money from her father to the French police at Le Havre, with an urgent request that Monsieur Warenghem should at once be asked whether it was true that he had sent money to his daughter. A French policeman was sent along to his home to interview him, and when he came M. Warenghem guessed at once that his daughter must be in some kind of trouble. But he could not know what Suzanne had said, nor what sort of answers he was expected to give the police. The policeman, understanding his dilemma, smiled sympathetically. "Monsieur," he said, "you look very tired to-day. Why don't you get a good night's sleep, and tell me your answers when I come back tomorrow morning?" Without saying a word, the policeman quietly left behind him on the table his copy of the German police report from Lyons, listing fully all the questions which had been put to Suzanne, along with her answers. The following day, M. Warenghem knew exactly what replies he was supposed to give—and a few days later, rather to their surprise and disappointment, the German police in Lyons received a report from Le Havre that the testimony of Suzanne's father agreed in every respect with what the girl herself had told them.

Then the Germans put another tricky question to Suzanne. "Why do you live in Marseilles? What have you been doing there all this time?"

At last Suzanne took refuge in the easy lie and with a well-assumed air of embarrassment, she told them. "The fact is— I have a lover there."

"Who is it?"

"I am sorry, that is something I cannot tell you. He is a married man, a prominent man in Marseilles. You can't expect me to ruin his life by giving his name away."

The German smiled understandingly. "Don't worry, we will not tell his wife."

With conviction, Suzanne replied: "No, I'd rather stay in prison than get him into any trouble."

Then they switched back to the point about her money.

"But if you have a rich lover, why do you need to get money sent by your father?"

"Because I don't like to accept money from my friend."

So it went on, Suzanne's battle of wits with the Germans. It went on for nearly two weeks, until somebody must have decided that more drastic methods were needed to make Suzanne talk. She was handed over to another team of questioners and its head, this time, was not a German but a hard-eyed French official who was working with apparent enthusiasm for the Nazis. And, between interrogations, Suzanne was kept no longer in a cell by herself in the St. Joseph prison, but in a large cell with forty or more women in it, criminals, prostitutes and resistance workers all mixed up together, crawling at nights with rats and bed-bugs.

Among the most good-natured of her fellow-prisoners Suzanne discovered, were the prostitutes. They indulged in no back-biting and were genuinely hurt when Suzanne hesitated to share in the generous food-parcels which were regularly sent to them by the men who had been their souteneurs. There was only one girl whom nobody liked: she was a farm girl in the prison awaiting trial for having murdered her baby and fed the body to the pigs.

"Now, Mademoiselle," said the Frenchman who had taken

over her interrogation, on the first day Suzanne was led in to him, "we want to know the names of all your friends. Listen to this list, and tell us which of these people you know." He put Suzanne in a chair with a blinding light in her face, and began to read out a list of people, not one of whom, as Suzanne realised, was in fact a member of the Marseilles network. Only one name she recognised, and it was that of a British officer working secretly in Nice. But she managed to give no sign of recognition when her questioner read that name, and he duly passed on to the rest. At the end of the list, Suzanne told him gently, "I am sorry, I have never heard of any of those people."

Now the Frenchman suddenly grew furious. He banged his desk so that the inkpots jumped from it and began calling Suzanne all the names in his vocabulary.

"Never heard, eh? Never heard, you dirty little slut. You 'don't remember' do you? Well, I'll have you put somewhere that may help you to remember."

He pressed a button on his desk and two men came and took Suzanne away. They dragged her down a corridor to a tiny cell, opened the door and literally kicked her inside. Then they slammed the door behind them. There was no window and no hole in the door. The cell was pitch dark and stinking. Suzanne fell on the floor, and fancied that she felt things creeping there. She has no idea how long she was kept there, because, almost as soon as she fell on the floor, she fainted.

Later that day the two men came and dragged her back to the interrogation room. The hard-eyed Frenchman was at his desk again. "Now, maybe you've had time to remember a few things," he said with a snarl. "We have another and even more unpleasant place we might send you to—but maybe your little stay in the cooling room has made you a bit more co-operative?"

Then the questions began again.

"Who are your friends, where do they live?"

"I don't have any friends except for my lover." It was not

a very good story, but the best Suzanne could manage on the spur of the moment.

Calmly the Frenchman rose from his desk, walked over and slapped Suzanne in the face twice, as hard as he could. Then he returned majestically to his seat, as though nothing had happened.

"Now, who are your friends?"

"I told you, I don't have any."

The room was in half darkness, with only a strong light playing on Suzanne's face. So she did not see what other men were present during her interrogation. But this time somebody came from behind her chair, and slapped her face again with all his force.

The questioning went on—and at least one of the questions they asked nearly made Suzanne, despite her pain and fear, laugh in their faces.

Weeks before, when she and Fernande had been sitting together one evening in Fernande's apartment indulging in girlish talk, Suzanne had told her friend of a brand of under-arm deodorant which she believed to be useful, and had written the name down for her on a slip of paper. The paper had been found by the police who searched the apartment after her arrest and now it was triumphantly waved in her face by her inquisitors.

"And what is the meaning of this?" they asked her. "This scrawl in your handwriting with the letters 'Odo-Ro-No'? It's obviously a code. What does it mean?"

"It's just a trade name, nothing at all," said Suzanne wearily. "Honestly it's nothing for you to worry about."

She got another slap across her face as her answer.

Suzanne received about three days and nights of this treatment—the pitch dark cell at night, and the slapping by day—and then quite suddenly it stopped. Suzanne never knew why. Her belief is that the report sent down to Lyons by the sympathetic police inspector in Le Havre, in which her father had confirmed the cover story which she herself had told, may have persuaded her inquisitors that she was at least partly telling the truth. She was sent back to St. Joseph prison, and she was not interrogated again. And as she sat, almost thankfully, in the cell at St. Joseph, wondering what was going to happen to her next, Suzanne comforted herself with the thought, "At least I have not talked, at least I haven't given in." Her will—and her pride —had not been broken.

Then, in the early days of March, one of the prison warders told Suzanne, "In a couple of days you are going to be transferred to Castres."

Suzanne knew what that meant. The little old-fashioned prison of Castres was being used at that time by the Vichy government as a hostage-prison specially for suspected members of the Resistance whom, for want of positive evidence, it had not been possible to bring before any sort of trial. From the ranks of those detained in its cells were taken from time to time Frenchmen who were executed at the demand of the Germans in retaliation for attacks made by resistance fighters upon them. The prison was run by Frenchmen, and conditions there did not rival in horror the enormities of Buchenwald and Ravensbrück. But, once in Castres, nobody could tell for certain how long they would stay alive.

In the St. Joseph prison with Suzanne was a Jewish girl with whom she sometimes talked about the possibility of escape. This girl had told her how once, when she had been arrested before, she had managed while being transferred from one prison to another, to elude her guard and jump from the train, which happened to be just outside the station of Montpellier. There she had made her way to a convent, whose nuns had taken her in and sheltered her for a considerable time. It was only later that she had been re-arrested. Suzanne now realised that the train which would take her from Lyons to the prison of Castres was also likely to pass through Montpellier station, and she obtained the name of the convent from the girl. Somehow she managed

Paul Cole: He was the Englishman in charge of the escape network for the Occupied Zone and the Forbidden Zone. To the many French men and women working with him in 1940 and 1941, he was the symbol of England still fighting against terrific odds.

zanne carrying her baby Patrick. Photograph taken in Marseilles by a street photographer in December 1942.

Left to Right: George Croise, Headwaiter, Monsieur Durand, owner of the "Chope du Pont Neuf" and Ely Lanty, Headwaiter. The three of them were first arrested on December 15th, 1941 and beaten up by the Germans who wanted to know where Paul was. Released two months later, they were again arrested in June 1944. This time it was Suzanne the Germans wanted to find; Monsieur Durand though tortured did not talk.

The restaurant in Paris where more than 100 escaped airmen and soldiers had a meal on their way to freedom.

to find out, too, the time at which her train would be due to approach that station, so she believed that she had a reasonable chance of herself making an escape.

On the day of her transfer, Suzanne was taken to the train by two policemen in uniform, handcuffed to one of them. Carefully she waited her time until she judged it to be about five minutes before the train was due at Montpellier. Then she asked the policeman to whom she was handcuffed if she might go to the lavatory. The man went down the corridor with her and was preparing to accompany her even inside, but Suzanne asked if he could not at least take off the handcuffs for a moment and wait for her outside. He agreed, but he insisted on keeping the door half ajar with his foot—and Suzanne found the window of the lavatory was fastened shut. While she was wondering what to do the train ran through the station. Her one hope of escape had gone, and by that evening she was sitting in a whitewashed cell of the prison in the old town of Castres.

*　　*　　*

Elsewhere in France, Paul Cole was on the move again, too. It was not long after the German occupation of southern France and Suzanne's arrest that the Nazi Security Police found him in the prison of Fort Monluc. There were still many members of the escape network whom they had not been able to track down, and they needed his help badly, especially as Suzanne had not talked. For some months they kept Cole in their own custody, moving him from one prison to another according, presumably, to where they most needed his special form of assistance. And Cole himself, saved by his German masters from execution by the French, seems to have co-operated with them even more enthusiastically than before. Official records estimate that throughout the war he betrayed a total of something like eighty Resistance men and women, of whom about fifty were in the end tortured to death or shot.

Finally, in the Spring of 1944, Cole was moved to the prison of Compiègne, where, having apparently by that time won the complete confidence of the Germans, he was released—and returned to Paris as a well-trusted German agent. Suzanne had not heard the last of Paul Cole even yet.

* * *

PART FOUR

With Head Unbowed

THE SOLID, seedy white building with the barred and boarded-up windows, which is the prison on the edge of the old market town of Castres, looks like a hard nut to crack for the gaol-breaker.

It stands in the narrow Rue du Palais, and adjoins the local Palais de Justice. Immediately opposite, during the war, was a post of the town's gendarmerie. The heavy green door which is the prison's only entrance, is double-locked and studded with nails. The gaol was originally built as a replica in miniature of the redoutable prison of Fresnes, outside Paris. Since 1956 it has been out of use and unoccupied, which was why, in preparing this book, I was able to visit it and inspect the lay-out in detail.

On that wet evening in early March, Suzanne, still handcuffed to the policeman, was led through the heavy green wooden door of the prison and handed over to the chief custodian, who duly signed a receipt for her safe arrival.

Immediately inside the prison's front door was a little white-washed hall, with, opening out from it on one side, a lodge in which a handful of prison guards lounged, smoked, gossiped and played interminable games of cards. On the far side of the hall was a grille of iron bars, kept permanently locked except to allow the passage of the guards themselves, or for the arrival or departure of prisoners. Through this grille Suzanne was taken, and up a staircase to the right which bore the legend, "Quartier des Femmes". Here, on the first floor, was a gallery running round all four sides of a great hall, with close wire-netting stretched all across the open space between the ground floor and the first storey. Some thirty cells opened out from the central hall on the ground floor, with a similar number opening from the gallery above. The women's cells were completely separated from those of the men below. Down on the ground floor was one cell, Number 11, which was marked outside "Cellule de Punition" and had a ring let in to the concrete floor to which a prisoner could be chained, and a heavily-padded door. There was a little chapel, surmounted by a cross, at one end of the great hall, and, next to the kitchen was cell Number 16, with four douches for the prisoners.

Suzanne's cell was like all the rest along the gallery, with whitewashed walls, a high arched roof and a window from which the view was obscured by bars and also by a board slanting outwards to leave only a small aperture through which the prisoner could see a thin line of sky. This was the only glimpse of open air that Suzanne could see. Sometimes the sky was cloudy, sometimes blue, and as she stared at it time and again in the days to come, that poem of Verlaine which she had loved in her childhood came back to her again:—

> Le ciel est, par-dessus le toit,
> Si bleu, si calme. . . .

Suzanne shared her cell in Castres with another woman prisoner, named Sabine. She was older than Suzanne and had been born in England of Belgian parents. After spending the first five years of her life in Britain, Sabine had gone to live in Belgium and she had dual British and Belgian nationality. Before the war she had run a picture gallery in Brussels and had later lived in France, from where, when the war came, she was repatriated. But immediately she arrived in Britain she had volunteered to go back to France as a member of that organisation which was variously known as "The Firm", "The Racket"

or, more officially, The French Section of the Special Operations
Executive of the War Office.

The "S.O.E." was organised early in 1941 to carry out
sabotage and espionage in German-occupied Europe and to
co-operate and organise the French, Dutch, Belgian and other
Resistance fighters who were even then beginning to make
themselves known. The French section, with its headquarters
in an imposing block of flats in Baker Street, was commanded
by Colonel Maurice Buckmaster, and it was under the auspices
of this organisation that Sabine had been trained and finally
landed, in the autumn of 1942 on the south coast of France, as
a courier for a British radio operator, Brian Stonehouse. She
had been captured near Lyons some time later, but she had
never told the Germans that she was a trained British agent of
the Special Operations Executive and they had still not been
able to pin any definite charge on her. So, like Suzanne, she had
been sent to Castres without any trial, there to await her further
fate.

Suzanne was glad to find somebody so agreeable to talk to,
and the two women settled down to a sojourn in Castres prison
which was to last all through that spring and summer. The life
in itself was rugged but not unbearable, yet the shadow of fear
hung constantly over the inmates of Castres, because nobody
knew who might be summoned at any moment, either for
execution as a hostage or for deportation to the concentration
camps of Germany and probable torture and death. Every
now and then a van would come and take somebody away—
somebody who was never heard of again. And even more
pressing than the fear of deportation was the constant gnawing
hunger, the urgent craving which all the prisoners felt for food,
for all of them at Castres, as in other French prisons at that
period of the war, were half-starved.

Sometimes a food parcel would be allowed to a prisoner who
had good friends outside. Once Sabine herself received a bulky
parcel and as she began to open it she and Suzanne already had

visions of a feast in their cell that evening. To Suzanne's disgust, the parcel proved, however, to have come from an art-loving friend of Sabine's who had sent her a packet of heavy illustrated books on modern art in the hope that these would console her in captivity. Suzanne had never liked modern painting, but now, viewing the uneatable volumes in hunger and disappointment, she hated it more than ever!

Life now fell into a fixed routine. The prisoners were woken at seven for "breakfast" which consisted of a mug of bitter barley coffee and a chunk of bread. Lunch was a plate of thin soup and bread and the evening meal another plate of soup. Once a week they got a tiny piece of meat and two lumps of sugar. Most of the day Suzanne and Sabine had to sit in their cells doing nothing. Virtually their only exercise was when one of them went to one of the small courtyards which opened out from the ground floor of the prison and where there were taps from which they could fetch water. It was while fetching water one morning that Suzanne encountered Boris the Yugoslav.

Boris had been a soldier of fortune for years. He had fought with the International Brigade in Spain, then got caught up with the Communist section of the French Resistance and had finally been arrested. That particular morning the surly, grey-haired woman wardress who usually accompanied Suzanne when she went to fetch water was not there, and she and Boris were able to talk for a few moments in whispers. Boris had not even known that there were any women prisoners on the first floor.

A week or so later Suzanne met Boris at the water-taps again, but this time she was caught talking to him by the wardress. The woman ordered Suzanne gruffly back to her cell and, as she was going upstairs carrying in each hand an old wine-bottle filled with water, gave her a powerful kick from behind which sent her sprawling on the hard stone steps, holding the bottles aloft to prevent their breaking. Suzanne to this day bears the scar on her knees from the gash she received when she fell.

But gradually, as the summer advanced, conditions in the prison of Castres grew easier. The surly wardress disappeared—the prisoners heard with delight that she was in trouble for having stolen prison food—and her place was filled by one of the male warders from the men's part of the jail. The food improved slightly and now included occasional plates of noodles, which were regarded as an enormous treat. The women's cell, formerly locked for the night at six, was now left open until nine. The guards even taught Suzanne and Sabine to play bridge, at first with cards hand-made out of pieces of cardboard, and later with a genuine pack smuggled into the prison. It seemed as though the guards themselves were supervised hardly at all. It was a blazing hot summer in the little southern French provincial town, and the war seemed a long way away. Outside, at bistros along the cobbled streets and avenues lined with plane-trees, the citizens of Castres lazily sipped their beer and *sirops* at open-air cafés; the general air of nonchalance spread even to the prison. For the fifty or sixty prisoners incarcerated there, this proved an unhoped for blessing.

And so it finally came about that on the stuffy evening of September 16, 1943, Suzanne and Sabine were sitting in their cell, clad only in their underwear because of the heat, idly playing cards, when there came a sudden knock on their unlocked door. Surprised, since it was not the habit of the warders to knock on prisoners' doors, Suzanne called out "Come in", and in walked the lanky figure of Boris the Yugoslav grinning broadly and with the light of excitement in his eyes.

"Come on, girls, we're escaping," Boris announced briefly. The two women were so thrilled at the news that they completely forgot that they were in their underwear, but leaped on Boris with exclamations of joy, and hugged him and kissed him until, grinning more broadly than ever, he interrupted them by telling them to get dressed as quickly as they could.

The escape had been well planned by some ingenious leader in the men's section of the prison. Urgency had been given to this action because of a report circulating in the prison that all the occupants were due shortly to be taken away and shot. Passing from mouth to mouth along the prisoners, the report said that in Toulouse already all the political prisoners had recently been removed and shot as hostages, and that Castres was next on the Gestapo list. So the plans for the great break-out were laid with great speed and efficiency.

Some of the prisoners had managed to smuggle in and hide arms, with the connivance of one of the guards who was secretly a member of the Resistance. With the help of the same man, duplicates were made of the keys both of the grille which separated the entrance hall from the rest of the prison and also of the great front door.

The action began around six o'clock in the evening, when half the prison guards had gone out for dinner, and only a handful of men were left behind. Stealthily opening the iron grille, which gave access to the guardroom, an "advance party" of prisoners suddenly attacked the guards, overpowered them and locked them in the nearest cell. Then they went round unlocking the cells and telling the other prisoners to join them in the hall.

So when Suzanne and Sabine, hastily throwing on their clothes, made their way down to the entrance hall, they found it crowded with excited prisoners waiting for the next stage of the operation. Everyone talked at once, until they were hushed by the men in charge.

Now there began a daring "mouse and cat" exploit to get the prisoners out in little groups without arousing the suspicions either of the remaining guards returning from their dinner or of the gendarmes sitting also at their evening meal in the post in the same small street and almost opposite the prison. Gently the front door of the prison would be opened for a moment, while two or three of the prisoners slipped out. Then it would be quickly closed again, while the prisoners behind it waited for the first party to slip away.

From time to time an unsuspecting guard, on his way back from dinner, would ring at the door. It would be opened to him—and a blanket would be thrown over him before he could see what was happening. Then he would be knocked on the head and thrown into the cell along with the other guards. The thick walls of the old prison effectively prevented any cries of the guards from being heard in the street outside. And luck was apparently with the escapers, for by good fortune none of the guards returned to the prison at the critical moment when one of the little groups of prisoners was leaving it. Altogether some fifty men, as well as Suzanne and Sabine, escaped from Castres that night.

The two women were pushed through the great green door after about twenty others had left and with them went a young Alsatian boy who had been put by force into the German army, had escaped, joined the Resistance and been caught. Quickly. and as unobtrusively as they could, the trio began walking through the streets of Castres just as dusk was falling.

They had no idea what direction they should take, for all of them had been taken to the prison in closed "black marias" and could not tell which were the streets which would lead them out of Castres. Their plan was to walk all night and if possible to reach Toulouse before dawn, for there they knew there were members of Resistance groups who would help them. By good fortune they hit upon a road which did indeed lead out of the town and seemed roughly to run in the direction of Toulouse. Actually, as it turned out, it was a secondary road, which led them a little too far to the south.

It was a nerve-wracking walk. The two women in their shabby clothes were so dishevelled that they feared that even their appearance would arouse the suspicions of anybody they met. They had, of course, no identity papers and only Sabine had a little money which she had somehow or other managed to secrete. German patrols on bicycles passed by, and every time the trio heard them coming they threw themselves flat into the nearest ditch and lay there until the Germans had gone past. After darkness had fallen, they walked on the grass verge of the roads so as to avoid making any noise, and later they walked across fields. They had no idea at what time was the curfew in that area, and they dared not be found walking after curfew and possibly questioned, since they had no papers. One group of four prisoners who failed to take all these precautions were in fact held up by police who questioned them for being out after curfew. They were discovered to be escaped prisoners, handed over to the Germans and, as Suzanne later heard, all tortured and finally shot.

There was also the anxious certainty that, as soon as the break-out from the prison was discovered, all the roads around Castres would certainly be sealed tightly by a police cordon. The hope was that the escape would not be found out until six o'clock the following morning, when a new shift of guards were due to come on duty. But in fact the discovery was made, Suzanne never knew how, at about two o'clock in the morning—and all roads within an eighty-mile circuit of Castres were sealed for a week or more afterwards.

As night fell, the trio made their way out to the open country-side, a gently undulating land of fields of wheat and maize and red-roofed farmsteads. Here and there they passed alongside little vineyards for, though the area of Castres is not a famous wine country, nearly every farmer in the district grows enough grapes to supply his own drinking needs.

Once, in the gathering darkness, Suzanne saw three men approaching, and she whispered a warning to the others to drop flat on the ground. But the men turned out to be fellow-prisoners also seeking their way to Toulouse, and the two parties joined forces and went on their way together.

They walked all through the night and when dawn came they had little idea exactly where they were. But across the fields they saw a little village, and they went down to the village church to ask the priest if he could help them. They felt confident that, whether he would help or not, the priest would in any case not denounce them. But as they knocked on the church door, all the dogs in the village seemed to start barking at once and, alarmed, the party made off into the fields again. They feared that every hand would be against them.

Walking on, they saw a convent and Suzanne and Sabine left the men behind them in an orchard, while they rang the bell at the great oak door. But when the sister opened it and saw the two disreputable-looking women, she almost slammed the door in their faces, and disconsolately Suzanne and Sabine rejoined the rest of the party in the orchard.

Further along the road that morning, they came to another village which the signpost told them was called Dourgne and here again they decided to try the priest. So they went inside the church and sat waiting there until the priest came in; then they told him frankly who they were. The good priest looked slightly alarmed, but promised to see what he could do to help. Soon after that he came back with a man who told them he would help to put them on their way to Toulouse—but urged that they must get out of the village quickly. He told them to meet him at noon beneath a stone cross on a path just outside the village.

But it was then only ten o'clock in the morning and the party had two hours to wait. In that time, as they hung around in the shelter of bushes outside the village of Dourgne their doubts and anxieties began to grow. Suppose the man was not really a friend? Suppose his real intention was to meet them, as he had said, at noon, but to bring with him a patrol of police? All the police stations in the area must have heard by now of the breakout from the prison of Castres and be on the watch for fugitives. In growing anxiety, the party decided not to keep the rendezvous by the stone cross, but to go on their way.

Outside the village of Dourgne the landscape rises into the heights of the range known as the Black Mountains, towering above the valley of Carcassonne. Up there, the party guessed, there would be living men of the Maquis who would certainly give them shelter. But it would mean a long and arduous climb— and a rough life among rough fighting men. After some anxious debate it was decided that the little party should break up; the men would set off for the Black Mountains and try to join the Maquis, the Resistance fighters who were already holding thousands of German troops at bay. Suzanne and Sabine would continue to seek shelter elsewhere. In any case, as members both of organised underground networks their orders were to get into touch with their colleagues as soon as possible.

So the men went off, and the two girls spent most of that day and all that night hiding in the bushes outside Dourgne.

The next morning, cold and hungry, they made for a little farm. They told the farmer's wife that they were two girl campers who had lost their way and that all their identity papers were in a tent somewhere in the countryside. As Sabine had some money to make a payment, they managed to talk the farmer's wife into giving them a good meal and allowing them to stay at the farm that night. But next day the farmer himself grew uneasy at the fact that, in time of war, he was sheltering two dishevelled-looking women with no identity papers and bluntly he asked them to move on.

But, in chatting the previous night, the farmer had happened to mention that there was a big Benedictine monastery not far from the village of Dourgne. Suzanne and Sabine had deliber- ately refrained from asking him for details, for fear that, if later he was interrogated, he would tell the police that he had directed them there. But after they were forced to leave the farm, they determined to try and find the monastery.

They did not dare to move around too much during the daytime. So throughout most of that day, although it was pouring with rain, they lay and sat in fields hidden by bushes waiting for darkness to fall. As soon as it was night, they set out to try and find the monastery. All through the night they

walked, sometimes discovering that they had been going round
in circles, and then, suddenly, at about five o'clock in the
morning they saw the great dark outline of the Abbey of
En Calcat, a little way up the hill from the village of Dourgne,
looming up before them in the moonlight. The two women
knew little of the ways of Benedictine monks, and had no idea
of what sort of reception they would get. But they were tired
and cold and dirty and hungry and desperate. No one could
have been in greater need of asylum. So they walked up the
gravel drive to the imposing front entrance of the monastery
and, with hope in her heart, Suzanne firmly rang the bell.

*   *   *

Suzanne had expected that, if anybody at all answered the bell
at the Benedictine monastery at that hour of the morning, it
would be an elderly, bowed and bearded monk. She was therefore pleasantly surprised when the door was opened by a tall,
slim young man, in full black Benedictine robes, with a lively
and friendly face. And she was even more relieved when she
realised that the dirty, wan and exhausted appearance of herself and Sabine was arousing on the monk's face an expression
not of repulsion or alarm, but of kindly sympathy.

"Could we see the Father Superior?" asked Suzanne.

Seeming to take in their situation at a glance, the monk
invited the two women: "Come inside," and quickly closed the
door behind them. He led Suzanne and Sabine across a large
tiled hall to a small whitewashed room leading off a corridor,
and motioned them to sit down at a table while he listened to
their story.

They told him everything and he asked many questions, and
then he went and fetched the Father Superior, who asked more
questions still. Suzanne realised later that the two men were
seeking to make certain that she and Sabine were not *agents
provacateurs*, trying to trap them on behalf of the Germans.
Finally the younger monk told them, "Yes, we can help you for

at least long enough to enable you to get in touch with your organisations." And from that moment, for just over three months, the lives of Suzanne and Sabine, who had suffered so much, became transformed by a period of rest, peace and Christian charity.

The Abbey of En Calcat, half-way between Albi and Carcassonne, is a great complex of modern buildings, all of local stone hewn from the nearby Black Mountains. It was begun in 1890, but work was suspended in 1903 on the disestablishment of the Church in France, and it was finally built between 1920 and 1939. Today it is a landmark for miles around, in the green, undulating countryside and always it has been a refuge for those in need of spiritual, or even material, help.

The young monk who had welcomed Suzanne and Sabine was Dom Emmanuel, the "Econome" or Major Domo, of the monastery, and thus he was in a position of sufficient authority to be able to take the decision to offer the two women shelter on his own responsibility and advise the Father Superior of his view. Dom Emmanuel was a man of merry countenance, whose austere life, devoted entirely to God from the time he was 18, seemed to have rendered him completely content. He had kindly eyes, a gift for lively talk, an open mind and a deep understanding of human nature. And for Suzanne he formed an immediate admiration. On the day I visited the monastery, years after the war, he invited me to sit at the mid-day meal in the great refectory where a hundred black-robed monks ate silently while one of them read a book in Latin at the end of the hall. And afterwards, walking in the cool, whitewashed corridors of the monastery and talking of the past, he told me: "I became full of admiration for the strength of spirit showed by both those girls. But Sabine, of course, was older, unmarried, and had not lost so much as Suzy. Yet Suzy told me, right at the start, that despite everything, she was quite ready to begin all over again. I found her admirable—*avec un courage de tonnerre*, the courage of thunder."

The two women, of course, could not stay in the Benedictine monastery itself. So later, on the morning of their arrival, Dom Emmanuel took them down the hill to a little two-storied house standing in an orchard not far from the main monastery building, but on the other side of the road, towards the village of Dourgne. This was "Bethanie", a little guest-house maintained primarily to accommodate relatives visiting nuns in the nearby convent—the one where the door had been slammed in Suzanne's face a couple of nights before—but also available to guests who wished to spend a period in quiet retreat. It was run by a gallant elderly Frenchwoman named Mademoiselle Marie-Thèrese de la Marguette, who had won many medals, through her services as a nurse in the First World War and later in Macedonia. She had the Frenchwoman's talent for combining capable common sense with a sort of stern good nature. She reminded Suzanne greatly of her own Tante Jeanne—and she promptly christened her "Tante". Assisting her was a trusted eighty-year-old servant named Anastasie.

That morning when Dom Emmanuel took Suzanne and Sabine down to Bethanie, he told Mademoiselle de la Marguette exactly who they were and from whence they had come. "But if there should be any trouble over them," he assured her, "I will take the full responsibility."

Proudly the elderly Frenchwoman replied, "Thank you, but I'm quite old enough to take on my own responsibilities myself. I'll welcome them with all my heart."

That is exactly what she did. She led Suzanne and Sabine down a clean-tiled corridor and upstairs to a spotless little room bearing the name "St. Paul" on the door—for all the bedrooms in Bethanie were named after the Saints. It was a simple country bedroom, with two old-fashioned wooden beds, plain pale blue distempered walls, a simple wash-hand basin and a little window looking out over lime trees and cherry trees. This room was to be their home for the next three months, but after their prison cells it seemed to the two women like Heaven

itself. Except when they went down to the little dining-room
of the guest-house (which they did when there were not too
many people around) Suzanne and Sabine ate most of their
meals in the "St. Paul" bedroom and hardly ever went out of
the house except after dark. They spent their days reading,
talking and listening, with Mademoiselle de la Marguette, to
the B.B.C. news bulletins. Just down the road from Bethanie
was the headquarters of the local gendarmerie—but the
gendarmes studiously refrained from asking too many questions
about the visitors to the monastery's guest-house. "They are
'*des gens très chic*'" as Mademoiselle de la Marguette assured
Suzanne. And when the two women tried to thank her for the
risks she was taking in sheltering them, she brushed them off
with the remark, "This is my way of serving in World War
Two—since I'm far too old to do anything better."

And whenever any chance caller did enquire about the identity
of Suzanne and Sabine, they were told that they were a mother
and daughter in need of rest and temporarily in Retreat. The
food, after prison fare, seemed to the two women a real consolation, for the local shops would usually provide a little meat
or butter for the two women who were, of course, at that time
without any regular ration cards. And at Christmas Dom
Emmanuel sent down to Bethanie from the monastery a special
hamper with honey, chestnuts and a chicken.

There were, of course, occasional moments of alarm, such as
the night when two Gestapo cars halted outside Bethanie and
two uniformed officers climbed out to inspect the building. But
they came to the conclusion that it was a farm, and drove on.

Suzanne, too, occasionally frightened even her best friends by
her readiness to take chances whenever she was bored. She
sometimes insisted on going out after curfew to climb the little
road to the monastery so that she could talk to Dom Emmanuel
in the "parloir" after the other monks had gone to bed. "I just
must talk to somebody," she explained, and she won the
respect of the monk by the very fact that she never pretended to

ut. Robert Sheppard:
achuted into France in
2, he landed on the roof
police station, and was
prison with Suzanne.

1941
Pilot Officer Oscar Coen,
R.A.F.

1958
Lt. Colonel Oscar Coen,
U.S. Air Force.

The young American pilot had crashed with his Spitfire
in the North of France. Suzanne escorted him to
Marseilles on his way to Britain in November 1941.

Left: Fernande and Roger Bertier with
their daughter. Cases of explosives were
found under their bed; Roger was in
prison with Suzanne, who was arrested at
their flat on February 2nd, 1943.

Below: The grim prison of Castres from
which Suzanne, Sabine and fifty men
escaped on September 16th, 1943.

Left: Don Emmanuel, one of the Benedictine monks who risked their lives to hide and help Suzanne and Sabine, and *right*, the Benedictine monastery of En Calcat

Left: Suzanne photographed after her escape from prison: she was only 21 but her hollow cheeks and sunken eyes made her look much older.

Below left: Capitaine Paul de la Taille: he was a member of the French networks for which Suzanne worked after her escape from Castres

Below: June 1944: Suzanne in the British Army training with S.O.E. to be parachuted back to France as a radio operator.

him to be more interested in religion than she really was. "I don't want to play a comedy just to please the Fathers," Suzanne once remarked—which, of course, pleased them more than any amount of false piety would have done.

Whatever Suzanne said, Dom Emmanuel listened sympathetically, and liked her lack of hypocrisy. One day Suzanne, who celebrated her twenty-second birthday at En Calcat, asked him with girlish disingenuousness, "Have you not ever wanted to get married yourself, Father?" Gently the monk explained that such sentiments were, indeed, a part of normal human nature— but that it was a part which Benedictine monks had decided to dedicate to God. Suzanne said no more, but her expression showed that this was a point of view which she did not find it particularly easy to understand.

And when there was not Dom Emmanuel there was always Mademoiselle de la Marguette to listen to Suzanne's problems and guard her with the tenacity of a tiger. Once, not long after she arrived at Bethanie, Suzanne announced to her newly-adopted "Tante"—"I really can't stand looking at my hair any longer—police or no police I've got to go to the coiffeur." Mademoiselle de la Marguette pointed out the unwisdom of Suzanne's showing herself in daylight in the village of Dourgne, but Suzanne stubbornly insisted. So the two went off to the local "Coiffeurs pour Monsieurs et Mesdames" on the village main street. By ill-chance, the chair next to Suzanne, who was having a shampoo and set, was occupied by the village gendarme. The man began to show an increasing interest in the girl beside him, for, despite all she had suffered, Suzanne had not lost her attractions. As time went on, the gendarme seemed to be becoming altogether too interested in the girl. So "Tante" de la Marguette broke in brusquely with "Monsieur, will you please cease forcing your attentions on my daughter"—and the gendarme somewhat sheepishly turned away.

Suzanne's life in this strange period of it, was indeed, an odd mixture of country repose and skirting on the razor's edge of danger. Once, during her stay at En Calcat, Suzanne heard that there was to be a big official ceremony in the monastery church, where the brother of Dom Emmanuel was to be installed as Father Superior. Both Suzanne and Sabine decided that they must at all costs be present. With some misgivings, Mademoiselle de la Marguette fixed them up with clothes and added black mantillas to cover their heads. So both the escaped prisoners went to the ceremony, which was attended also by the Commandant of the Gendarmerie, with all the civil and military officials of the area and their wives. Suzanne, with characteristic impudence, insisted on taking a seat well up in front, and found herself in fact seated just behind the wife of the Police Prefect of Castres.

But apart from such diversions as these, Suzanne and Sabine were, of course, more seriously occupied with the question of what to do next and how they could best get into touch with their own networks so as to receive further instructions. The first thing they did after their arrival at En Calcat was to give to Dom Emmanuel the names of the contacts which they had in Marseilles, Toulouse and Nice, and he sent one of the monks, Father Hilaire, to both these cities, to try and deliver a message. But the two women had been long in prison and the addresses they had given appeared to have become out-dated, for Father Hilaire returned to report that he had not been able to find any of the people mentioned. All had apparently either moved— or had been arrested.

Sabine had an address in a neutral country and, by a roundabout route a message was sent there, asking that news of the women's whereabouts should be sent to the War Office in London, who should be requested to remit their instructions.

Simultaneously the monks themselves had been in touch with a French resistance organisation, one of whose leaders was Colonel du Noyer de Segonzac, who at that time was hidden in the region of Toulouse organising the Maquis in the neighbourhood of Castres. He agreed to help and summoned one of his liaison officers, handsome Captain Paul de la Taille, to meet him in Toulouse. He told the Captain succinctly; "We've two women to smuggle over the Pyrenees. Get them some good shoes and some warm clothes."

"Fine," said Captain de la Taille, "but how big are the women, and what size shoes do they take?"

"No idea," replied his chief. "Go up to En Calcat and fix that all up yourself."

And so it came about that one December day, sitting in their little room at Bethanie, Suzanne and Sabine received a message from the Captain telling them to meet him a few days later at the nearby railway station of Castelnaudry, from where they could together catch the train to Perpignan. On hearing which the incurably romantic and optimistic Suzanne exclaimed, "Hurray, we'll both be in London for Christmas!" Dom Emmanuel agreed to drive the women over, hidden in the back of a little utility truck belonging to the monastery. Alas, the rendezvous misfired, for the truck with Suzanne in it arrived at the station just two or three minutes after the train for Perpignan had left. Dom Emmanuel himself drove the party all the way to Toulouse, from where, travelling in the corridor of a train packed with Germans, they were able to reach Perpignan that night.

The town of Perpignan, the nearest one of consequence to the Spanish frontier, was alive with every sort of Vichy and German police. It was a dangerous place for escaped prisoners to hang around in, so Captain de la Taille went without delay to the man who was in charge of the frontier crossings for his network, and told him that Suzanne and Sabine needed to get to Spain in a hurry.

"Are you mad?" asked the man. "Two women? Why, they'd never make it. Come, I'll show you something."

And in an adjoining room he showed them five American pilots who had just turned back to Perpignan, having failed in their attempt the night before to reach Spain. The man explained that all the easy routes across the Pyrenees were now so heavily patrolled that it was useless even to try them. The hard but less supervised route necessitated fording a deep and swift-running river—and this was mid-December. One guide and one of the pilots had almost been drowned the night before. "Come back next summer, and maybe we could try again then," the frontier expert told them.

Disconsolately the party returned to the refuge of Bethanie and discussed what they should do next. It was Captain de la Taille who suggested that the two girls should go to Paris and work there for the Resistance, at least until such time as their return to Britain should be arranged. From the Captain Suzanne heard with delight of the growing extent to which the Resistance had become a power in France since the period when she herself had been in Marseilles and in prison, of the regular flow of information which the Resistance organisations in the cities were now sending to Britain, of the sabotaging of German arms, supplies and communications. Gladly the two women agreed to go to Paris as soon as possible. They had appreciated the kindliness and peace of Bethanie—but they were delighted at the prospect of seeing some real action again. Anything, Suzanne felt, was better than brooding over the past.

The Captain took Sabine and Suzanne to a photographer's and had pictures taken for their identity cards. Suzanne's face, thinner and with sunken eyes, looked very different now from how it had done in the light-hearted days of 1941 when she had been photographed in Paris with Tommy Edgar and Jimmy Tobin, before their first journey south.

And by a strange coincidence the man who organised the false identity papers for Suzanne and Sabine, at the request of Captain de la Taille, was Monsieur Oberg, the Chef de Cabinet of the Prefect of Police of Toulouse—the very man who had, only three months earlier, ordered the police barrage on the roads around Castres, following the news of the prison break-out. A few nights later Captain de la Taille took Suzanne in to Toulouse and, with a pleasant sense of irony, invited Oberg to dine with them both. He presented Suzanne to the police official; "This is one of the unfortunate victims whom you tried to catch on the night of the big escape."

With a gleam of amusement in his eye, Monsieur Oberg asked Suzanne, "A pretty girl like you—however did you get among a gang of people like that?"

Suzanne spent one night in a safe house belonging to friends of the Captain in Toulouse, and the next day she travelled to Paris. It was a journey which took her once more into great peril. And it was in Paris that she heard, for the first time for over a year, further news of Paul Cole.

*   *   *

When Suzanne arrived in the dour, bitterly-cold Paris of December 1943, she was tired, anxious—and doubly on the run. She feared recapture by the Germans; but even more she feared that Paul Cole would find her again. She knew that he had disappeared from Fort Monluc after the Germans had occupied southern France and that he must therefore once more be at large again and doing the work of his German mentors. And she realised all too well that, in view of his plot to rid himself of her in Lyons, he had turned decisively against her. So, during the three months she spent in Paris before leaving for Britain, she slept in different houses as often as she could—and slept with a revolver under her pillow.

"If Paul walks in on me I shall shoot him at once," she told a friend at this time. "I won't give him time to talk." And who knew better than she the dangers in that glib tongue?

Suzanne had wanted, on the first night of her return to Paris, to stay with Tante Isabelle, because Tante Jeanne was at that time away in the country. But she did not dare to do so for fear that her aunts, all three of them, might already have been denounced by Cole, or that at least he might come seeking her at their apartments. So she slept the first night with relatives of Captain Paul de la Taille and only next day went cautiously out to Becon-les-Bruyères to see if all was well with Tante Isabelle.

But Suzanne's arrival in Paris had happened to coincide with one of the greatest bombardments of the capital by the American Air Force. Aimed at the industrial targets of Levallois and Courbevoie, the raid caused havoc in the surrounding residential centres. When Suzanne reached the station of Becon-les-Bruyères she found the area a chaos of shattered buildings and broken glass and was firmly stopped by a police cordon. She was unable to reach her aunt that day. Some of the worst of the bombing seemed to have been just around Tante Isabelle's flat. So, greatly anxious, Suzanne slept that night in a little hotel and next day succeeded in getting through the debris to Tante Isabelle's apartment. She found her aunt without gas, electricity or water, and with every window of her flat shattered, but otherwise unhurt. The old lady was thrilled to hear at first hand the story of Suzanne's adventures and together they exchanged all they knew about Paul Cole. But Tante Isabelle agreed, "It's better you don't stay here with me at present—Cole knows my address too well." So Suzanne moved on, and slept again in a different house that night and succeeding ones.

She warned everyone she could in Paris to beware of Paul. But when she went over to her good friends the Crépels, the two girls, Jeanne and Francine, thought she had gone mad, and so did old Monsieur Crépel himself. "Why," he said, "Paul Cole used to lunch here with us regularly. Seemed a real English gentleman to me. You must be mistaken, Suzanne."

"Oh, please believe what I'm telling you," urged Suzanne. And it was not long before the Crépels had reason to change their minds.

Only a few weeks later a young man who belonged to a French Resistance network came to the Crépels with bad news. "Paul Cole has been set at liberty by the Germans," he told them. "We know he is somewhere in Paris and he is looking for Suzanne. Tell her to be very careful."

Promptly Francine Crépel bicycled across Paris to Tante Isabelle to pass on the warning, and, hearing this news, Suzanne intensified her precautions. Would Cole, she wondered, succeed in finding her? Would the whole story end with her having to shoot him with her own hand?

Through January, February and March, Suzanne, in contact always with Sabine, waited on in Paris for news of whether, when and how she could succeed in getting to Britain. Meanwhile, she volunteered through Captain Paul de la Taille to do work of any sort for the Resistance networks with which he was in touch. Years later, when I talked to the Captain, now an officer of the Supreme Headquarters Allied Powers in Europe, about this period he told me, "I think our group in Paris was a comfort to Suzanne at this time. She was still full of patriotic ardour and I was always astonished at her courage. But I think the work she did for us gave her consolation in her dismay about Cole and the loss of her son. She needed to be kept busy—and she was."

In those three months Suzanne did work at one time or another for at least five different Resistance networks, taking messages, conducting escapers, translating B.B.C. news bulletins, and forging documents, for which she claimed to have a special talent. Often she acted as a "look-out", keeping watch for the Germans outside buildings in which Captain de la Taille and other Resistance chiefs were meeting. She ran many risks and had many narrow escapes, once avoiding disaster only because she happened to miss a train.

That was the time when she was asked to pick up a party of American Air Force pilots from the Chateau de St. Maur, near Tours, where the owner Madame de Poix regularly hid allied airmen who were waiting a passage home. Suzanne, always punctual by habit, went to the Austerlitz station in plenty of time, but found when she got there that there was an enormous queue at the ticket office. Fuming, she stood in line, but the queue moved interminably slowly, and before she could buy a ticket Suzanne saw her train for Tours pull out of the station. She was in a state of frustrated fury when she reported back to Captain de la Taille.

"I'll have to go by the next train," she told him.

"No, Suzanne, I think you'd better not go at all," he replied. Captain de la Taille explained that while Suzanne had been at the station he had been trying several times to get the Chateau on the telephone to inform them—in a guarded form of code language which he used—that Suzanne was on her way to pick up the six pilots. But he had been unable to get any answer. This struck him as ominous, because the Chateau was occupied by several people and at least a couple of old servants and at such an early hour in the morning there certainly should have been somebody to answer the telephone.

"I'm afraid something has gone wrong," he told Suzanne. "Stay in Paris until we can check."

The Captain's caution probably saved Suzanne's life. For in fact Madame de Poix had been denounced, and she and all the pilots had been arrested. The local priest, who had helped her, was also taken by the Germans at the end of his Mass one Sunday; he was deported and died. If Suzanne had reached the Chateau that day she would certainly have found the Gestapo waiting for her.

Another of Suzanne's tasks at this period combined both humourous and dangerous aspects in about equal proportions. She was asked to take to a secret airfield near Chateauroux— where Lysanders from Britain were now regularly picking up clandestine passengers—a Resistance chief from Eastern France who had been aided on his way by M. Francois, of the famous restaurant of the Gare de l'Est in Paris (the only station restaurant to have a double star in the Guide Michelin). But the Resistance chief, like M. Francois, was a connoisseur of good living, and when Suzanne came to pick him up for the journey she found that he had been celebrating all too well his impending departure for Britain. Clutching small Suzanne by the arm, the heavy man reeled into the train that was taking them south, sang merrily on the journey, and Suzanne dreaded that at any moment he would proclaim to all their fellow-passengers the real purpose of their journey. She quietened him as much as possible and changed the subject as often as she could; but she was greatly relieved when they finally reached Chateauroux.

Suzanne worked so hard during this period in Paris that her health, which had improved somewhat at the Monastery, now began to deteriorate seriously again. She looked increasingly pale, drawn and haggard, so that her Resistance colleagues became seriously alarmed about her. One of them, named Raoul, had parents with a big castle in the country and he suggested that Suzanne should spend a fortnight with them, so that she could have a rest and good food. So down to this chateau, in the Rhone valley, Suzanne went and the whole family, including Raoul's thirteen brothers and sisters, did all they could to restore Suzanne to health and happiness. They gave her breakfast in bed, took her for walks in the country, made her special dishes, tried to get her interested in all sorts of things to take her mind off the war and all she had been through. When she left, she felt a different person. But she never saw again those good friends who had shown her so much human kindness. The Chateau was, in fact, being used by the Resistance as a secret depot for arms. And later that year the Germans discovered this. One day German armed men turned up at the Chateau looking for one of Raoul's brothers whom they suspected of working with the Maquis. When they did not find him there, they took Raoul instead. They shot him in front of his parents and all the children and then set fire to the Chateau. It was months later that Suzanne heard about this, and by that time she was far away in Britain.

When at last, her Resistance colleagues knew that the time was approaching for Suzanne to make her own trip to Britain, they welcomed the chance to send important documents along with her. One of them, Jean Maurichaux Beaupré, a former air force officer who was working for the de Gaulle organisation on preparations for the allied landings, asked Suzanne to meet him in the Tuilleries gardens where he gave her a precious roll of microfilm containing about fifty pages of information on the Atlantic Wall collected by the French actor Gilbert Gil. Suzanne agreed to take it, and it was arranged that the microfilm's safe arrival in Britain should be announced by the B.B.C. with the cryptic words "Onesime a une belle bobine"—a play on words since in French slang bobine means not only a roll of films but also a face.

Another agent asked Suzanne to take with her a plan of a German radar station at Jouy-en-Josas which needed to be bombed as soon as possible. But Suzanne was warned that on no account must the plan be discovered if she was captured by the Germans, because only one person at Jouy could have given it to the Resistance; discovery would mean for him certain death. Suzanne agreed to take the plan—provided it was put onto really thin paper. With memories of her first arrest in Lyons she explained, "I've already had to eat one of those things."

Then finally, towards the first week of April a message came to Suzanne and Sabine from the War Office in London. It was the long-delayed answer to the message they had sent via a neutral country long ago when they had been together at En Calcat. It told them that they should come to Britain as soon as possible, and that arrangements were under way for their transfer. The efforts which Suzanne had made ever since 1940 to reach England were now at last, four years later, to be rewarded. And she even received a small amount of pay.

Both women were delighted. Sabine bought herself a bottle of Chanel No. 5 perfume. Suzanne celebrated by buying herself two of the few things which could still be obtained in Paris without clothing ration cards—a filmy black transparent nightdress, and a brown hat with a white feather. The rest of the money she blued on a bang-up lunch to her Resistance friends in a Chinese restaurant in the Latin quarter. Wine circulated freely. At the next table to them was a German naval officer, resplendent in his full uniform. Full of bravado, and with a vague hope that they might be able to extract from the navy man some useful information to take to England, they invited the German officer to join them. He was delighted, but spoke little French.

"Does anybody here speak English?" asked the German.

"I do," said Suzanne, and for the rest of the dinner she chatted gaily with the German, inserting here and there what seemed to her a subtle question about his naval affairs. The German was amiable—but discreet. He yielded no information and finally bade the rest of the party a cordial farewell. Ruefully Suzanne told her friends, "I guess I'm just no Mata Hari."

On April 10, Suzanne and Sabine left for the coast of Brittany —only to hear when they got there that the British naval craft which was to have taken them across the channel had left the night before. They had missed the boat. There was nothing for it but to return to Paris for a few days. Again a safe hiding-place was found for Suzanne by Captain de la Taille. Then word came through that a new attempt was to be made.

On the night before her second departure for Britain, Suzanne had a farewell dinner with Captain de la Taille at a restaurant near the Place Victor Hugo. They had lived through a tense period together, and they celebrated their separation with some emotion on oysters and white wine.

"So you see the last of Paris, and those German b . . ., and say good-bye to everybody, including me," said Paul de la Taille.

"Don't worry," said Suzanne with a light in her eye which seemed to be fired both by excitement and determination. "I'll soon be back again, you know."

"And how shall I know whether you have arrived safely in England?" asked the Captain.

"By a special message on the B.B.C." replied Suzanne, "and I chose it myself; it will be '*Patrick fait toujours pipi au lit*'."

The journey to the Atlantic coast had, by 1944, grown extremely perilous. The Germans were expecting the Allied invasion and had tightened security precautions everywhere. The whole coastal area had been declared a "zone interdite", and nobody was allowed to be there except the local inhabitants, who were closely watched. So, on the night of April 14, 1944, Suzanne and Sabine, a guide and three American pilots travelled by train to a point in Brittany just outside the forbidden zone. There they were taken to a little grocer's shop and hidden for an hour or so in a back room of which Suzanne remembers no details except that it contained a huge mound of fresh butter, such as she had not seen in France since the beginning of the war. Then a baker's van came to collect them for the perilous trip into the "zone interdite."

The gallant baker had smuggled scores of Resistance people into the coastal zone in his van, and the principle he used was the simple one advocated by G. K. Chesterton's Father Brown—that some things can be so obvious that they are never seen at all. The roads were watched, the trains were checked, any lorries with closed doors were stopped and searched. So the baker used, for smuggling his clients, a little bread delivery-van which had no rear doors at all, only a widly-flapping loose tarpaulin over the back. The German sentries never supposed that anyone would have the nerve to smuggle clandestine passengers in a van which was not even closed and, through all the trips the baker made, nobody ever looked inside. So, behind a pile of sweet-smelling loaves, Suzanne, Sabine and the three airmen crouched, and held as firmly as they could to the sides of the van as it rattled and swayed over the little Brittany roads. To make the trip seem even more convincing, the baker stopped on his regular rounds in the villages delivering his bread. Once, while he was carrying loaves into a little village shop, Suzanne was terrified to hear the unmistakable crunch of Wehrmacht boots on the pavement. The steps ceased just near the van, and Suzanne held her breath. Even her beating heart seemed to make a terrific noise. But the German soldier had stopped only to light a cigarette, and passed unsuspectingly on again.

The van drove on, finally reached the coast and drove straight into the garage of a fisherman's house, somewhere north of St. Brieuc. When the garage door had been closed, the party were allowed to get out and were taken into the house. There Suzanne found a regular "Cooks Tour" of passengers for England. There were at least sixteen people, men and women, and even one boy of fourteen, who had been smuggled in previously by the baker and were due to cross the Channel that night in the same ship of the British Navy. Never had Suzanne seen anything better organised. The fisherman's wife had a fine meal of roast pork, potatoes and red wine for everybody, and after the meal Suzanne and Sabine felt so content that they both went to an upstairs room, lay down and slept. There was only one mishap. Sabine broke her precious bottle of Chanel perfume and the smell of it spread over the whole house. Suzanne and Sabine tried everything to wash it away, but still the perfume remained —and everyone finally agreed that this must be the most exotic-smelling fisherman's house in all Brittany.

As evening fell, all the party in the house gathered round the radio set to listen to the B.B.C. news bulletin in French. It had been agreed that a code sentence, read at the end of the bulletin, should tell them whether the ship in which they were to cross was able to keep its rendezvous with them that night. There was a tense moment as the news bulletin ended and the announcer began to read the code messages. But finally they heard the message they had all been waiting for; they were due to leave that night.

Around ten o'clock that evening the team of escapees left for the three-hour walk to that point of the beach at which the rendezvous with the British Navy had been made. It was in fact at Plouha. Suzanne insisted on wearing the new hat she had bought in Paris, tying it securely on her head with a dark scarf, and receiving a good deal of teasing for her elegant appearance at such an adventurous moment. As the party left the house, a number of revolvers were handed round. The fisherman explained that, if a passing German patrol came upon the party in the dark in the "zone interdite" there would be no choice but to shoot it out with them. The orders were: "If there is any trouble kill as many Germans as you can before you get killed yourself. And if by chance you do not get killed, there will be a rendezvous for all survivors at the Paris Métro station Passy—next Friday afternoon at three and every Friday afternoon after that for the next ten weeks."

So they started on their way, walking in single file in the darkness, about eighteen escapers bound for Britain, two or three Breton guides and half a dozen local volunteers who went to the beach to help unload the arms, ammunition and radio sets of the agents who simultaneously were due to be landed by the Royal Navy that night. They walked mile after mile across wild moorland, where every bush looked in the darkness as though it might be a human being. Every quarter of an hour or so, the chief guide halted the column to pause and listen. Faint sounds of the night came to their ears, sometimes a footfall, which made the men in the party grab on to their revolvers. Suzanne kept the film in her pocket and held the plan in her hand ready to eat it if there was any trouble. But every alarm proved to be false, and finally, around one o'clock in the morning, the party reached the cliffs above the tiny cove where they were scheduled to meet the Royal Navy one hour later.

Suzanne tore her stockings to shreds, scratched her legs and ruined her skirt in the scramble down the steep cliff-side, and around her everyone else was slithering, falling and grunting with oaths which, by orders, had to be suppressed. Finally the whole party was assembled on the beach in the darkness, not talking, not smoking, hardly daring to move for fear of making a sound, and staring through the night to see who could first catch a glimpse of any naval craft. After what seemed an eternity of waiting, the guide exclaimed in a whisper, "There they are—I can hear the engines." Nobody else had heard a sound, but sure enough a few minutes later several dinghies, rowed by shadowy figures were seen approaching the beach. There were whispered exchanges, men splashed in and out of the sea carrying packages—and suddenly two powerful arms gripped Suzanne and a voice which could belong only to a British sailor said, "You come along with me, Miss. You don't want to get those pretty feet of yours wet." The gallant sailor carried Suzanne through the waves, and deposited her in his dinghy—where she found herself sitting anyway in about six inches of water.

Soon after that, the boat rowed silently out to one of two Motor Gunboats which had kept the rendezvous that night, and Suzanne scrambled over a net and on to the deck. She and her companions were led silently below to a cabin which, for security, was in pitch darkness and for some time they stood bunched together there, hardly daring to move, since they could see nothing around them. Then they heard the low throb of the ships engines and knew they were on their way. Only a few minutes after that, the lights in the cabin went on and a sailor appeared with a tray. "'Ere yer are," he said in a Cockney voice which was also music to Suzanne's ears, "I've brought yer a nice cup of tea."

But the tea party did not last long. On that mid-April night the Channel was unkind and soon the ship began to roll and plunge in a way that sent the teacups flying and Suzanne hastening to lie down. After having survived so many hardships, she suddenly found herself laid prostrate by seasickness. And when, some time later, she heard a fusillade of shooting going on somewhere aloft, as the motor gunboat was attacked by some German vessel in mid-Channel, she felt too ill even to care. But, soon after dawn that morning, the Royal Navy, escorted by the R.A.F., finally took Suzanne Warren safely in to Dartmouth harbour—the end of her four-year-long journey to Britain.

A few nights later two special messages duly went out over the French service of the B.B.C. One told Jean Maurechaux-Beaupré that his "bobine" had arrived safely. The other was Suzanne's very personal one, *"Patrick fait toujours pipi au lit."* The Three Musketeers heard it, sitting at their radios in the little Paris apartments. Captain Paul de la Taille heard it, in the lodge of a concierge in the Rue d'Orsay who nightly put her radio set at the disposal of French Resistants. The Crépel family heard it and rejoiced. Presumably the Gestapo heard it too, and wondered what it meant.

And down in the village of Dourgne, Mademoiselle de la Marguette, who had heard from Suzanne before her departure, chanced to stop in at the local chemists' shop just as the pharmacist was remarking, "What terrible nonsense les Anglais do sometimes talk on that radio of theirs. *'Patrick fait pipi au lit'*—what in the world do they mean?" But the old French lady knew very well—and hurried up the hill to tell the good news to Anastasie and the Benedictine monks.

But entering war-time Britain, even under official orders, was not the simple matter that Suzanne had supposed. She was welcomed by British officials with friendship and a bunch of red roses. But all the same she spent ten days in being interrogated, checked, and examined by British Intelligence Officers, who had, of course, to make certain that she was indeed Suzanne Warren herself and not a German agent who had learned her story and was trying to pose as her. Finally all was declared in order and, on April 27, she was handed a very special pass by an Immigration Officer testifying that now, ten days after she had actually landed, she had at last officially entered Britain. The form itself was coldly official. It said; "The bearer, Suzanne Henriette Warren, has been landed in the United Kingdom on condition that she . . . registers with the police and does not engage in any kind of employment without the consent of the Ministry of Labour, and leaves the United Kingdom not later than such date as may be specified by the Secretary of State."

Which seemed to Suzanne a little severe seeing that her only intention now was to get herself trained and parachuted back to France at the earliest opportunity.

*　　*　　*

It must have been early in 1944, not long after Suzanne's arrival in Paris that Paul Cole, being by now completely in the power of his German captors and having largely won their confidence, was finally, at the prison of Compiègne, given a measure of provisional freedom. The German conditions for this were simple: merely that he should use this freedom to return to Paris and complete as rapidly as possible his task of denouncing those of his former friends whom he had not already betrayed. And above all that he should deliver to them Suzanne Warren, whose escape from their clutches seems particularly to have irritated the Gestapo.

But at this stage of the war, members of the Resistance were better informed about Paul Cole than he was about them, as is indicated by the early warning of his return to Paris which was given to the Crépel family, and through them to Suzanne. Paul had no success in his intensive search for the woman whom he had made his wife.

And now the sands were running out for the Germans. The Allied invasion of Normandy began on June 5th, and obviously there was no time to be lost if Paul was to complete his work of betrayal. The Germans must have been pressing him hard to show some positive results.

It may seem strange that at this late stage of the war the Gestapo should have thought it worth while devoting their efforts to rounding up Resistance workers whose main activities dated from a much earlier period. Perhaps the reason lies in a combination of the traditional Teutonic fury and desire for revenge when their dreams of conquest had been shattered, and

M

a quite normal military desire to put out of the way as far as possible all those people who might constitute a danger to German security behind the fighting lines at this moment of intense crisis for the Wehrmacht.

However that may be, there now came to be played out by Paul in Paris a series of scenes similar to the ones he had already staged nearly three years earlier at the home of the Abbè Carpentier and Monsieur de Fliguë. And the first of his chosen victims was the Crepél family, at whose comfortable flat in the Avenue de Suffren he had so often been a welcome luncheon guest, and who had so willingly supplied him, whenever he had asked for them, with false identity cards.

It was Monsieur Crépel himself who related to me what had happened on that sunny morning of June 30 when Paul Cole turned up so unexpectedly at his flat.

"Just after seven o'clock in the morning," he said, "our front door bell rang. I was in my pyjamas when I opened the door and found Paul Cole standing outside. He looked a very different man from the gay, self-assured Cole whom I had last seen. He had always dressed impeccably, but now his clothes were shabby, his trousers uncreased and—funny how you notice these things at such a time—when he came in and sat down I saw there was a hole the size of a franc in the sole of one of his shoes.

"With Cole was a man whom he presented to me as an American officer. 'He's an agent of the United States Intelligence,' Cole said. 'Can you help him in the same way as you've helped so many others, and get him false identity papers?'

"Suzanne had warned me about Cole. So I played stupid and pretended I didn't know what he was talking about."

The two Crepél girls, Jeanne and Francine came in while Cole was talking, and they heard him tell their father, "But you can't leave this man in the lurch; you've simply got to help him to escape, like you always did before."

Francine came to her father's aid by pretending to misunderstand what Cole was driving at.

"I suppose you want us to get your friend some ration cards," she said—for by this period of the war nearly everyone in France would get extra cards if they could. "We might possibly be able to help him, I suppose."

"No, no," said Cole. "You know that isn't what I mean at all."

While all this was going on, the supposed American officer said very little, but Monsieur Crépel noticed that he kept looking surreptitiously at his watch. Finally the man leaned across to Cole and whispered something, of which Monsieur Crépel caught the words ". . . the address of your wife."

So that was it. Paul Cole was still on his determined hunt to track down Suzanne and, having failed elsewhere, was now trying to locate her through the Crépels. Monsieur Crépel had heard the B.B.C. message announcing her safe arrival in Britain, but now all he said to Paul was, "My dear Paul, the last time we saw her she was with you."

"No, but you *must* tell me," urged Paul. "It's terribly important to me."

And now came the next scene in the comedy which Cole and the Germans had obviously rehearsed and timed carefully beforehand. There was a new ring on the door, a knocking, and the cry of "German police—open up."

Monsieur Crépel, still not quite positive about Paul's real position, quickly motioned to him and his companion to hide themselves behind a door leading to the kitchen. Jeanne, in her dressing-gown, opened the door and saw two men in the long grey mackintoshes that were almost a uniform for Gestapo agents in civilian clothes, each with a revolver in his hand. Jeanne tried to shut the door, but one of the men pushed it open, and flourished an identity card.

"You are hiding two spies here," said one of the men. And he pushed his way into the corridor leading to the kitchen where Cole and the "American" had been standing without making any attempt to leave the flat by the back door, as they easily could have done. With a semblance of roughness, the two Gestapo men put handcuffs on Paul and his companion. Said Cole, "You see, it's all up with us now. But I am sure if you will just give us the address of Suzanne nothing will be done to you."

Then, suddenly, the "American" took charge. He shook off his handcuffs and started to interrogate the whole family. Finally he said, "Get dressed, pack your suitcases quickly; you will have to come with us."

The two daughters pleaded for their parents. Francine said, "We'll come with you, but please leave father and mother out of this. They knew nothing about anything we were doing."

To her surprise, the Gestapo man suddenly packed up his notebook and said a few words in German to the others. "Very well," he said. "I will leave you for the moment—but, remember we know that you did provide people with false papers."

They maintained the pretence with Paul Cole to the last. As he was led away in handcuffs, Cole turned to the Crépels in one final appeal. "Look," he said, "*Je suis fichu* (I'm sunk); I beg you only, just for my sake, to give us the address of Suzanne." The Crépels never saw him again. To Monsieur Crépel, it seemed apparent that he had now become just a pawn in German hands.

Having failed at the Crépels, Paul now led his German masters to another of his good and faithful friends—Monsieur Durand of the Chope du Pont Neuf, who already had been once arrested and released.

Only a few days later, Paul Cole walked into the brasserie accompanied, as usual by two men whom he presented as allied airmen. Monsieur Durand was absent at that moment, but Georges Croisé the waiter was behind the bar and Cole ordered beers for himself and his companions from him.

"By the way, Georges," said Cole, "have you seen anything of Suzanne lately?"

"Not since I saw her with you, Monsieur Cole," said Georges guardedly.

After only a few moments of conversation, the two companions of Cole revealed their identity. "Police Allemand" they announced, "you are under arrest."

They forced Georges Croisé to take them to the house in which Monsieur Durand was living and there arrested him. As they did so, Cole turned apologetically to Georges Croisé and with a sheepish attempt at a smile said, "Sorry, old man, it's just the luck of war, you know."

The Germans took Eugene Durand, who was then over sixty, to their dreaded torture headquarters in the Avenue Foch and there submitted him to every sort of physical violence, including the torture of La Baignoire, the ice-cold bath into which the victims were thrust and held under the water until they nearly drowned. And time and time again all they asked him was "Suzanne—where is she now?" But Monsieur Durand told them nothing, and after eight days he was released again— a semi-broken man.

After dealing with Monsieur Durand, Paul went on to two more of his former good friends. First, with his German associates, he visited Julien de la Tour, the head waiter of the restaurant in the Boulevard St. Michel who had been at his wedding. M. de la Tour and his wife were both arrested and sent to concentration camps.

Then Paul turned on a woman, Agnes Kirman, who had hidden so many pilots for him in her apartment in the Rue Quatrefages where de Fliguë and Professor Holweck had been arrested. He had Madame Kirman taken away—and used the occasion to appropriate for himself some of the most treasured articles in her apartment. Madame Kirman was ruthlessly questioned, beaten, and transported to Ravensbruck concentration camp, where she died.

Down at St. Martin-le-Beau, too, M. Besnard, who had helped so many of Cole's men across the demarcation line, was arrested and taken away to captivity in Germany from which he never returned.

But now the Battle of Normandy had been won and the Allies were already driving on towards Paris. The Security Police were destroying their papers and hurriedly packing for Germany. And Paul Cole went with them, driving his own little red car along with a German convoy. He was apparently already far away by August 25, when General de Gaulle triumphantly entered Paris. But even now the last had not been heard of him, and his nimble wits were still to serve him well in his personal battle for survival.

* * *

Meanwhile, back in Britain, Suzanne was having a happy and hectic time—happy in her celebrations of the Liberation of her country, and hectic in the training she was undergoing to be parachuted back. She could hardly wait to go as she heard with mounting excitement of the allied advance through one French city after another and the great work of her Resistance friends, who, by mid-August had themselves liberated eight departments in Brittany and the south, had brought traffic in the Rhone valley to a standstill and had freed Toulouse, Hendaye and almost the entire Lyons district. Such achievements as these by her compatriots filled Suzanne with pride.

She pestered her chiefs of the Buckmaster organisation to press on with her training for her return to France. She did a week in a commando school, trained as a radio operator, and did ten parachute jumps, though every time she felt almost sick with fear just before she jumped.

But the war went too quickly for her. By the time she had finished her training her unit was disbanded. And finally Suzanne returned to France not by parachute, but as a member of the Free French Army in a convoy which landed her, at the end of December 1944, by a strange coincidence, on the beach of Le Havre—the very spot from where her long odyssey had begun.

Once more she climbed the familiar hill to the house in which her father lived. The war had aged and tired Monsieur Warenghem greatly. Part of the time he, too, had spent in prison, for he had been charged with helping in the disappearance of a consignment of nickel desperately needed by the Germans, and his well-known anti-German views had made matters worse for him. But he looked with admiration at Suzanne's smart new uniform and all the temperamental clashes which father and daughter had once had were forgotten as he held her affectionately in his arms as he said, "My dear stupid daughter, what have you been doing all this time?" It was only three months later that Monsieur Warenghem died.

Suzanne was in Paris for the first wonderful New Year's eve celebrations after the Liberation, and her three aunts could hardly believe that the smart and soldierly-looking young woman was the same girl as the one they had seen only nine months before looking like a hunted animal on the run.

One of Suzanne's first acts after it became possible to travel freely in France again, was to journey south to arrange to put a proper headstone on the grave in Marseilles of baby Patrick. And here she made a strange discovery. For Suzanne reached the graveyard and found the simple wooden cross which marked the baby's resting-place. But when she looked in the registration book kept by the cemetery guardian, she saw that a special mark had been made in the margin of the book alongside Patrick's name.

"What does that mark mean?" she asked the official.

"It means that somebody came here and made a special enquiry about your baby, Madame," the man replied. "Who? The Gestapo perhaps—I cannot say."

Suzanne shuddered slightly. Could it have been Paul Cole?

*   *   *

The mystery of the mark in the cemetery register was never explained. But Paul Cole was indeed at large again. And of all his bold and impudent exploits nothing excels the ingenuity with which he sought to extricate himself from the predicament in which he found himself as a result of the allied victory.

In May Hitler had died, the Wehrmacht had collapsed, the Gestapo had disintegrated. Paul Cole found himself suddenly on his own in Germany, with no masters now, only fellow-workers of the German Sicherheitsdienst—the Security Police —as anxious about their own future as he was about his. But his subtle, supple brain was not long in finding an ingenious solution to his plight.

With him at that moment was one of the Germans with whom he had collaborated most closely, the notorious Sturmbann-fuehrer Kieffer, who during the war had operated in the French section of the Sicherheitsdienst in the Avenue Foch, in Paris. Ostensibly, after all that Cole had done for Kieffer, they were colleagues: but in such a relationship where could confidence lie? As the allied armies closed in ever more threateningly towards Germany, Cole (as it became known to British intel-ligence officers later) became increasingly anxious about Kieffer's intentions towards him. Would the German, at the last moment, throw him after all into a concentration camp, now that he had served his purpose, now that there was nobody left for him to denounce? Would he even, perhaps, suddenly "liquidate" him altogether, an an inconvenient witness? Cole must have brooded on this problem for some time before he came up with a typical solution.

On the characteristic principle of "I'll look after you, Jack, and you look after me," Cole finally proposed a deal to Kieffer. It was that the two of them should together surrender to the nearest available regiment of the American Army.

"I'll tell them that I'm a British officer whom you have helped," explained Cole. "And I can certainly get you a safe-conduct and complete clearance. And I'll be sure to get on all right with the Americans."

Kieffer readily agreed to the plan. And so it happened that one day in the early Spring of 1945 Cole, in civilian clothes, walked into the headquarters of an American cavalry regiment in Southern Germany, asked to see the Squadron Leader and introduced himself with an air of authority.

"I'm a British officer," he said as he heartily shook hands. "Captain Mason is the name. I've been acting as an agent here in Germany and just waiting for you chaps to turn up. Very glad to see you, I'm sure, and I may be able to be of service to you, I think. By the way, this man Kieffer has been very helpful to me, so I'd be glad if you can do anything for him."

Conditions in defeated Germany were fairly chaotic at that moment, and incidents such as this were not exceptional. The Americans threw open the hospitality of their mess to Cole, gave him a uniform with a Captain's badges of rank, and soon had him co-operating enthusiastically with them—interrogating German prisoners. Cole was now in his element. By an ingenious turn of the tables, he was able to denounce to the Americans, unfamiliar and in a strange land, many of the Gestapo chiefs with whom he had himself associated. From information which he gained while expertly interrogating prisoners, he was able to lead his new hosts to the places where the Germans had secreted the art treasures which they had looted from occupied countries, and even to their hidden stores of wine and liquor. He was given a desk in an office of the C.I.C. (Counter Intelligence Corps) and by all who knew him at the time he was voted a "regular guy".

Later, Cole decided to move his sphere of operations to the French zone. So one day he just walked out of the C.I.C. office taking with him a supply of American Army notepaper and official rubber stamps, and turned up at a French headquarters in the little town of Alsthausen, south-west of Ulm.

Looking immaculate in his new American uniform, he marched boldly into the office of the French Commandant de la Place. "Bonjour, mon Commandant," said he, saluting smartly, "I've been sent here as your American liaison officer. Anything I can do to help, you know. . . ."

With his official credentials, which he had himself manu-factured, and his self-assured manners, the French had even less reason than the Americans to suspect Cole. He installed himself comfortably at a farmhouse outside Alsthausen, and continued his work of interrogating Germans in a nearby prison camp. He was *persona grata* with everybody. He entertained Allied officers freely, at well-organised parties, lavishly supplied with liquor "liberated" from the Germans. At that moment it must indeed have seemed to Paul Cole that his long and treacherous story might well have a happy ending.

But two things finally proved his undoing: the long arm and long memory of British Intelligence—and his own over-confidence.

For months previously, back at the War Office in London, intelligence officers had been building up, from reports of those who reached Britain from occupied France and from other sources, a clear picture of the true activities of the man who had called himself sometimes Harold Cole, sometimes Paul Delobel or Paul Deram. In view of his treachery, it was made a point of honour to track him down as soon as possible. But how to find a man who might be anywhere, under any name, in all chaotic Europe?

In the end it was Cole himself who gave to British Intelligence the one vital clue they needed. Flushed with his new success, he wrote a post-card to a former associate of his—who had never lost confidence in him, had obstinately refused to believe that he was a traitor. The card, bearing the address from which he was operating and signed with the old familiar name of "Paul", was aimed at reassuring his friend that all was well with him. But the address on the card was carefully noted by a British Intelligence Major to whose hands it was passed.

Promptly a member of a British Army intelligence unit in Paris, Major Hope, set off, with a French police official, in a car for Alsthausen. They arrived at the office of the French commandant, in a little villa just off the main street, and asked if he knew where they could find "le Capitaine". "Certainly," said the Commandant, "I was with Captain Mason myself only last evening. He gave a most successful cocktail party; we all went along, and even a British general was there." When Major Hope explained the true identity of the Captain, the French Commander was flabbergasted. But he agreed to send a message to Cole asking him to come down to his office as soon as possible, on the grounds that he had a "new job of interrogation" for him to do.

Cole arrived in a jeep with two American officers, and under his arm he nonchalantly carried a tommy-gun—as many people did in newly-occupied Germany at that time. Major Hope announced his identity and said, "You are Harold Cole and I have come to take you back with me."

"Nonsense," said Cole, at first trying to bluff it out, "I don't know what you are talking about."

But as one of the French officers moved towards him, he suddenly raised his tommy-gun. Major Hope closed in on him just as the gun blazed out, and he got a bullet through his leg, but he grabbed Cole and rolled to the ground with him, rolled beneath a grand piano which stood in the Commandant's sitting-room. It was under the grand piano that Cole was finally overpowered, and then he was led, dishevelled and protesting, to Major Hope's car, and driven back to Paris.

The British authorities were taking no chances. They wanted to be sure that they had got the right man. So not long after Paul's arrival in Paris a telephone call was put through by the British Air Attaché at the Paris Embassy to the French 342 Squadron (Groupe Lorraine) in Holland. There, Roland Lepers, Paul Cole's early associate on the escape route of Northern France, who had later escaped himself to Britain, was now serving as a pilot. "Come at once to Paris," Lepers was told, and, somewhat mystified, he flew down the following day. When he arrived, a car met him and he was driven to a villa on the outskirts of Paris. "We've got Paul Cole," a British officer informed him. "Come and identify him."

There, in the basement, Lepers saw Cole again for the first time since the series of denunciations in Lille. And now Cole looked an abject figure, very different from the dashing and self-confident man who had so often eaten and drunk with Lepers at tables alongside German officers in the cafés of Lille.

"You know I never did you any harm, old man," pleaded Cole as he recognized Lepers in his air force uniform. "You don't kick a man when he's down, eh?"

Lepers turned away. "That's Cole all right," he told the British officers. "But remember he's a clever and dangerous man. You'd better be careful he doesn't escape from you."

"We'll take care of that, never fear," the officer assured Lepers with a slightly superior smile.

Cole was transferred to the SHAEF Allied Military prison in the Caserne Mortier, near the Porte des Lilas, run jointly by the British, American and French. There he was seen and identified, too, by another of his old associates on the Marseilles escape route, Dr. Donald Caskie, the heroic Scottish priest. When Dr. Caskie came face to face with Cole in his cell at the Caserne, Cole stoutly maintained, "I don't know who you are; I've never seen you before in my life."

"Well, I know who *you* are," said Caskie. And he told the prison guards, "Keep a good eye on that man, he's a clever devil."

And Dr. Caskie, too, was assured, with a self-confident air by the prison official that there was nothing whatever to worry about.

But it was not very long after that that Suzanne, still in Paris doing work in aid of Resistance members returning from concentration camps, heard the astonishing and alarming news; "Paul Cole has escaped from prison."

And indeed he had. With his remarkable gift for ingratiating himself with people, Cole had won the confidence and friend-ship of the British and American guards.

One day Cole asked if he could have a typewriter in his cell, so that he could spend his time "writing out a full confession". This request was granted. And when, a few days later, he com-plained that his cell at nights was so bitterly cold that he found it hard to type, he was allowed to move himself and his type-writer to the warmth of the prison guard-room. There, one evening, he was peacefully typing, and chatting amiably to the guards, when an American Sergeant walked in and hung up his jacket on a peg alongside the hook on which Cole's own jacket was hanging. Cole saw his chance—and acted. He asked per-mission to go along the corridor to the lavatory on his way back to his own cell. Casually the guards agreed: they were used to Cole's presence there in the evenings. So quietly Cole tucked the typewriter under his arm, took the Sergeant's jacket from its peg and put it on. Then he unobtrusively walked out—not to the lavatory but to the prison gates where, showing the identity papers contained in the Sergeant's pockets, he was allowed to pass through, typewriter and all, unchallenged. It was one of the most undramatic prison escapes in history.

For Suzanne, the news of Paul's new escape was alarming. She had an unreasoning fear that he would try to find her, might even now attempt to do further harm, perhaps to herself, perhaps to her aunts. Cole seemed to be a perfect example of a split personality, and who could say what such a disordered mind might conceive? So once again, in those dark winter days at the end of 1945, Suzanne slept with a revolver under her pillow. She knew for certain that if ever Paul walked in on her he would not give her a chance to telephone to the military police.

Meanwhile a new life, which seemed full of promise, was developing for Suzanne herself. Back in Britain at the parachute training school she had met a handsome and lively American, of French descent, who was training like herself to be dropped in France as a special agent. Now he, too, was in Paris as an Intelligence Officer for the American Army, and Suzanne realised that she was deeply in love with him. But she wished with all her heart that the spectre of Cole could be removed once and for ever from her life. He had done her such wrong that he had become a kind of obsession with her.

Somehow the past still seemed to haunt her. Among the survivors struggling back from the concentration camps whom Suzanne was helping as best she could at her office in Paris were a number of victims of Paul Cole, among them Madeleine Deram, who had returned from Ravensbruck only just alive. Uneasiness grew in her mind as, day after day, there was no news from the military authorities of where Cole might be. He seemed to have outwitted them completely. They had circulated his description and photograph to all police stations and army depots in France, so far to no avail.

Cole had, indeed, found a new refuge for himself, and a new protector, a new woman to victimise.

Madame Pauline Herveau was a fifty-one-year-old French widow, mother of three daughters, who kept a little establishment known as Billy's Bar in the Rue de Grenelle, just off the Boulevard Raspail. One day in late November Paul Cole walked into the bar, and bought himself a drink. He told Madame Herveau that he was an American soldier named Sergeant Carpenter, in Paris awaiting demobilisation, and very lonely. Gradually he won her confidence, and confessed that he was a deserter. The good-natured Frenchwoman agreed to give him shelter. Paul Cole moved into a room above Billy's Bar, and stayed there right through Christmas. He rarely went out except at night, and his meals were taken up to his room by Madame Herveau, who also provided him with clothes and gave him presents.

Cole's hope apparently at this time was that he could continue to take refuge with Madame Herveau until his troubles blew over or he could find some way of escape from France, perhaps from Europe. For now four different countries had at various times been hunting him—Britain for desertion and treachery, Germany for having escaped from the Gestapo, France, for the betrayal of Resistance men and America for his escape with a typewriter from the Caserne Mortier after having hoaxed the American Army.

And indeed Cole, with his gift for self-preservation, might have succeeded in biding his time quietly with the hospitable Madame Herveau—if only the neighbours hadn't talked. But people began to grow increasingly curious about the foreigner who lived above Billy's Bar and never went out except after dark. One day one of them called in at the local Commissariat de Police at the St. Thomas d'Aquin station, and suggested that they ought at least to check the man's identity papers.

The police themselves had no idea at this time who the stranger at Billy's Bar might be. Just as a matter of routine they sent over an officer to ask the concierge for details of Mme. Herveau's lodger. Cole was out at the time, and when he came back and was told by the concierge that someone had been making inquiries about him, he remarked with an air of apparent casualness, "Yes, I know somebody is after me but I'll be gone soon. I'm catching a train to Brussels in a few hours." Then, turning to Madame Herveau, he said, "Come on, Chérie, let's have a glass of champagne."

That delay was fatal to Cole. A few hours later, on the evening of January 9, 1946, two detectives, Inspector Coty and Inspector Levy, came back to Billy's Bar and asked Madame Herveau about her guest. She called quickly up the stairs to Cole, "Chérie, it's the police." The two detectives rushed up to the first floor and burst into Cole's room. He was standing with his back to the window as the police entered, flourishing a revolver in his hand. He fired three shots, wounding Inspector Coty in the shoulder and the right arm.

The police withdrew for a moment, and snatched their own

revolvers. And then a strange thing happened, which cost Cole his life but which at least reflected on him, in the few seconds before he died, one final moment of decency. As the two detectives came into the room again, the figure of Madame Herveau came between them and Cole, directly in his line of fire. If he had shot at that moment he might have killed the detectives, but he would almost certainly have shot the elderly Frenchwoman as well. In a momentary access of chivalry, Paul hesitated to fire. That second of hesitation was fatal to him. From behind Madame Herveau the guns of the two policemen blazed out, and Paul Cole fell forward from the window, dead.

But even at that moment, the French police did not know whom it was that they had killed. When they searched Paul's pockets, they found the American sergeant's identity card which he had stolen before his escape from the Caserne Mortier. It was only after checking with the military authorities that the realisation came that the elusive Cole had been caught at last. He was just over forty when he died.

From Belgium Pat O'Leary was flown down to identify the body. Major Hope identified it too. From the Chope du Pont Neuf old Monsieur Durand was taken to the Paris morgue for a last sight of Cole. And M. Crépel, calling at the local police station, was shown a photograph of the man they had shot which he recognised as being Paul Cole.

*　　*　　*

But Suzanne knew nothing of the events in Billy's bar until the following morning when, sitting at breakfast in an American Officers' mess in Paris she opened a London newspaper and saw the four-column headline: "Police Shoot Man Four Armies Hunted," with beneath it a picture which was unmistakably that of Paul Cole.

That should have been for her the end to all her anxieties, the moment when all the accounts with the past had at last been settled. But Suzanne had grown so used to thinking of Cole as elusive and indestructible that even then a nagging shadow of a doubt persisted in her mind. Was the man they had shot really Cole beyond a peradventure? Why had they not called her, who had known him so well, to identify the body? Would he even now perhaps turn up again to plague her life? Such suspicions seemed totally illogical, yet they did persist as a faint cloud in Suzanne's mind. And when, years later, Tante Jeanne was found dead alone in her Paris flat, although the doctor who was called had not the slightest doubt that she had died from heart failure, Suzanne again was momentarily gripped by the old fear—could her aunt's death have been caused by Cole?

Much happened to Suzanne in the years which followed. She married her handsome American and lived with him first in California and then very happily in London. Gradually the shadow of Paul faded from her mind. But I think it was not finally and forever dispelled until Suzanne came back to Paris again and sat with me one wet Friday afternoon at the Café de la Gare, somewhere down in that desolate area of the shunting yards behind the Gare de Lyon.

Outside in the rain heavy railway lorries rumbled by, and half-torn Communist posters flapped dismally in the wind. Inside the café, blue-overalled French workers sipped red wine and stared with interest at the slim figure, the abundant brown hair, the intense and lively face of Suzanne, still an incongruously attractive young woman in those dismal surroundings.

And there was an old friend from Suzanne's past, Georges Croisé, the waiter from the Chope du Pont Neuf, and the only survivor from the restaurant, since Monsieur Durand had died a year before. Georges Croisé poured out three bottles of light French beer and sat down with us at the marble topped table and, as he raised his glass, said with a wry smile, "À la votre, Suzanne. I thought you were dead."

And Suzanne, with a flash of that gay defiance of spirit which had somehow made her indestructible throughout her Resistance activities and the agonising personal ordeal which had resulted from them, smiled back and said, "Well, Georges, I'm really still here, you see."

And then we asked Georges Croisé about the end of Cole, and he told us the final story of how Monsieur Durand had been called to identify the body and had actually seen Cole lying dead in the mortuary.

"There was no doubt about it at all?" asked Suzanne, with an apparently casual air.

"No," said Georges Croisé firmly. "Monsieur Durand had not the slightest doubt that it was Cole."

And now at last it was clear to Suzanne that she had nothing more to fear from life, that every trace of the menace which had once hung over her had gone.

No longer need she be plagued by those recurrent small anxieties which had remained obstinately with her ever since her Resistance days—the fear of sitting in front of an uncurtained window at night, the fear of the postman's knock, the fear of being followed, the fear that somewhere, sometime, the tall stranger she saw passing in a street would suddenly prove to be Paul Cole.

Now, if she thought about the past at all, she need remember only the heroism and the good comradeship of the patriots who had worked together, and the days when hearts had been young and naive and completely loyal. Time and again life had dealt her blows which might have shattered completely anyone not of strong courage. But now she was through it all and out on the other side.

*　　*　　*

Epilogue

IF the story of Suzanne Warren has a moral it is, surely, that courage, physical and moral, and steadfastness do sometimes bring their own reward and that, in the words of the poet quoted by Sir Winston Churchill at the height of the war, "If hopes were dupes, fears may be liars."

For at least the labour and the wounds of Suzanne Warren were not in vain, as anyone can see who today visits her happy London suburban home and meets her two irrepressible sons.

Some others whom we have met in the pages of this story have also emerged with success from their war-time ordeals. Ian Garrow is alive, in Scotland. Dr. Donald Caskie can be heard preaching every Sunday in the Scottish Kirk in Paris. Roland Lepers, now married to a beautiful English girl whom he met in the Royal Air Force, is a business man with a pleasant home at Garches, outside Paris. Bob Sheppard, who shared the horrors of Dachau with both Pat O'Leary and Brian Stonehouse, is also doing well in business in Paris, where his neat, bristling moustache convinces many Frenchmen that he is the original likeness of "Major Thompson". Sabine, too, is alive and well, and now runs an art gallery in London.

Suzanne's first two "football players"—Tommy Edgar and Jimmy Tobin are flourishing. Edgar is a District Officer in Kenya.

On the 24th August 1944, Suzy received the following letter from Tommy Edgar, then serving in India.

"I feel I must write to you on this day of days, when Paris and Marseilles have been liberated. I had tears in my eyes as I listened to the news and I am so very glad both for France and for you. I am so happy that les Forces Francaises de l'Interieur managed to do most of the work. It is a triumph for them and will repay all their days of suffering and misery. It also shows the world that the French were never beaten, that la France was never crushed. Ever since I came back from France I have argued fervently that the French would rise to a man (and to a *woman*) when the time came and they have done so. You must feel so proud to have had such a share in this moment and I suppose you are sorry you can't be there to see it. So am I!"

Tobin now owns a successful ironmongery business in Dunbartonshire. Years after the war, Suzanne was happy to make contact once again with Tobin and his Scottish wife, Mary. Tobin wrote her a long letter from his home in Scotland recalling their war-time adventures together. He wrote:—

"How can I ever say thank you for all the trouble and risks you and Roger Pelletier took for Tommy and myself. I often thought of you and him and the four of us on our long trip from Paris, and, my, how lucky we were to have such brave and willing companions.

I always remember the scene at the railway station when all of us were detained prior to crossing the demarcation line. What a moment! And how thrilling it was, even the sticky bits. . . . When I told my family (long after 1941) and my other friends, they just could hardly believe that there were brave people like your good selves left in the then torn world.

Again, let me say how grateful I am for all the things that you have done for Tommy and me. I was happy to learn of your further adventures, and praise God, your eventual escape and rescue. . . .

I myself returned to Normandy with the Invasion Force,

and I had the great pleasure of visiting some of my old French comrades friends in Rouen. . . ."

And Tobin added the information that Roger Pelletier had also come through the war without mishap and was married now, and living near Paris.

Others, too, can record a happy ending to their war-time trials. Madame Deram, now restored to health after her concentration camp ordeals, manages a pleasant little café with her husband at Loisons-sur-Lens. The fact that such people as she, Vladimir de Fliguë, Bob Sheppard, Dr. Caskie and others could survive their war-time ordeals and still return to normal post-war lives is, like the story of Suzanne herself, a testimony to the powers of survival of the human spirit.

Monsieur Louis Triffe of the D.S.T. in Lyons, who first arrested Suzanne and Paul Cole, now lives in retirement. Suzanne's two friends in Lyons, Roger and Fernande Bertier, are the prosperous owners of a flourishing laundry-business outside Paris, and if you travel in a couchette of the French National Railways it is probable that the pillow-cases you use will have been laundered by them. Their daughter has Suzanne as her godmother.

Others concerned in this tale were less fortunate. Apart from those whose deaths have been recorded earlier on in these pages, Monsieur Duprez, of the Mairie of La Madeleine died also, and to-day a plaque to his memory, erected by the British Legion, can be seen on the brick wall of his widow's little house in the Rue de la Gare. Mario Prassinos and Dr. Rodocanaci both were finally arrested and perished in German captivity. And the fifty or more other brave people who died as a result of their friendship with Paul Cole are remembered by their families, honoured by their countries and duly named in the official archives.

As for Cole himself his story, though macabre, is something more than that. Clearly his was a highly complex character.

Counterbalancing to some extent his final treachery is the fact that he undoubtedly did genuine and valuable work in setting up and helping to run the escape route for British soldiers and pilots. Would he have gone straight if he had avoided capture? Why did he commit the ultimate meanness of robbing the three aunts who had gone out of their way to help him and nurse him through an illness? The answers to these questions can never be given now.

Little is known of the origins of Cole. There is no doubt that he was unfortunate in his early life, and, perhaps through unemployment in the hard 1930's, he fell into bad ways. And when the testing time came it was the yellow streak which became dominant in his character. The result is a story surely unparalleled among the many extraordinary records thrown up by the Second World War.

*   *   *

Just as this book was going to press I received an interesting recollection of Cole from an Englishman, now naturalised French, Mr. Ernest Swan, who lives at Marcq-en-Barceul. Mr. Swan had lived near where Cole was billeted in the months before the fall of France. Then in October 1940, in the words of Mr. Swan "I was walking along the rue de Lille at La Madelaine, when I passed a civilian. I got an awful shock when I recognised Cole."

After some conversation Cole informed Mr. Swan that he had been taken prisoner but had escaped and had then got in touch with the Intelligence Service who had sent him to Lille to collect all the British soldiers he could and get them through France to Marseilles.

"He then explained to me that his main job was to get rations and clothing and then travel with the soldiers to Paris. He then suggested that as I was a resident in France I could help him to collect clothes and so on, and that is how I began working in collaboration with him."

"I must say that until his arrest by the Germans Cole had done some very good work: he was untiring, always on the go, nothing was too much trouble for him. He of course had a French identification card and he had also a typewritten letter in German stating that he was deaf and dumb. . . . One way he used this letter was when he got news of some soldiers hiding in villages around Lille he would get on to the road leaving Lille for that destination and stop the first German lorry going that way; he would show the chauffeur the letter and mark on the lorry with chalk where he wanted to go, and he usually obtained satisfaction and was conveyed to his destination. He would then obtain some civilian clothes for the soldiers in the village and bring them back to Lille by using the same methods. We often had some good laughs over this, wondering what the German soldiers would have thought had they known that they were conveying British soldiers. Once in Lille, they were handed over to Madam Deram who kept house for them at 50 Avenue Bernadotte, La Madeleine, and who looked after them like a mother, washing their clothes and so on. She was a wonderful woman."

Mr. Swan was present in the Avenue Bernadotte on the morning of Cole's arrest, and saw him being taken away. He says "As he left, I vowed that after the war I would let it be known in England what work he had done."

Later Mr. Swan was warned about Cole by a British officer, but Mr. Swan concludes his account by saying "Cole was undoubtedly an adventurer, and a bad lot, but nevertheless let us say that he had a little streak of humanity in him."

It seems fair that the last word on Cole should be, thus, a charitable one spoken by a former colleague.